WAGES FOR STUDENTS *was written and published anonymously during student strikes in Massachusetts and New York in the fall of 1975 by three activists associated with the journal Zerowork.*

SUELDO PARA ESTUDIANTES *fue escrito y publicado de manera anónima por tres activistas vinculados a la revista Zerowork durante las huelgas estudiantiles en Massachusetts y Nueva York en el otoño de 1975.*

DES SALAIRES POUR LES ÉTUDIANTS *a été écrit et publié anonymement pendant les grèves d'étudiants du Massachusetts et de New York à l'automne 1975 par trois militants associés à la revue Zerowork.*

Wages for Students | Sueldo para Estudiantes | Des salaires pour les étudiants

Introduction | Introducción | Introduction © 2016 George Caffentzis, Monty Neill, John Willshire-Carrera

This book is an editorial collaboration published and distributed in North America and South America | Este libro es una colaboración editorial, publicado y diseñado, en América del Norte y América del Sur | Ce livre est une collaboration éditoriale publiée et diffusée en Amérique du Nord et Amérique du Sud © 2016 Common Notions with vaticanochico and Éditions de l'Asymétrie.

Edited by | Editada por | Éditée par: Jakob Jakobsen, María Berríos, and Malav Kanuga.

Collective Spanish translation | Traducción colectiva al castellano | Traduction collective vers l'espagnol: Catalina Valdés, Carlos Labbé, Mónica Ríos, Romina Pistacchio, Constanza Ceresa, Javier Osorio, Catalina Donoso. Special thanks to Carolina Alonso Bejarano for editorial assistance and Edison Pérez for Spanish proofreading.

Collective French translation | Traducción colectiva al francés | Traduction collective vers le français: Alponse Girard, Frédéric Racine, and Paulin Dardel of Éditions de l'Asymétrie. Special thanks to Adrien Tournier of Éditions Entremonde and Gabrielle Gérin for editorial assistance.

ISBN: 978-1-942173-02-1   LCCN: 2015954298

Common Notions   vaticanochico
131 8th St. #4   Obispo Donoso 24
Brooklyn, NY 11215   Depto 5 Providencia
commonnotions.org   Santiago, Chile
info@commonnotions.org   vaticanochico.com

Éditions de l'Asymétrie
38 Rue Fabre d'Eglantine
Toulouse, France 31000
editionsasymetrie.org
editionsasymetrie@openmailbox.org

Design and typesetting | Diseño y tipografía | Conception et exécution graphique: Morgan Buck and Josh MacPhee | Antumbra Design www.antumbradesign.org

Printed in the USA by | Impreso en Estados Unidos por | Imprimé aux Etats-Unis par: the employee-owners of Thomson-Shore www.thomsonshore.com

WAGES FOR STUDENTS

SUELDO PARA ESTUDIANTES

DES SALAIRES POUR LES ÉTUDIANTS

WAGES FOR STUDENTS

English | inglés | anglais [1]

SUELDO PARA ESTUDIANTES

Spanish | castellano | espagnol [67]

DES SALAIRES POUR LES ÉTUDIANTS

French | francés | français [139]

EXAMINATION BOOK

_____

_____

_____Section_____

_____Date

_____

wagesforstudents

WAGES FOR STUDENTS

WE ARE FED UP WITH WORKING FOR FREE
WE DEMAND REAL MONEY NOW FOR THE SCHOOLWORK WE DO.

WE MUST FORCE CAPITAL, WHICH PROFITS FROM OUR WORK, TO PAY FOR OUR SCHOOLWORK. ONLY THEN CAN WE STOP DEPENDING ON FINANCIAL AID, OUR PARENTS, WORKING SECOND AND THIRD JOBS OR WORKING DURING SUMMER VACATIONS FOR OUR EXISTENCE. WE ALREADY EARN A WAGE; NOW WE MUST BE PAID IT. ONLY IN THIS WAY CAN WE SEIZE MORE POWER TO USE IN OUR DEALINGS WITH CAPITAL.

WE CAN DO A LOT WITH THE MONEY. FIRST, WE WILL HAVE TO WORK LESS AS THE "NEED TO WORK" ADDITIONAL JOBS DISAPPEARS. SECOND, WE WILL IMMEDIATELY ENJOY A HIGHER STANDARD OF LIVING SINCE WE WILL HAVE MORE TO SPEND WHEN WE TAKE TIME OFF FROM SCHOOLWORK. THIRD, WE WILL RAISE THE AVERAGE WAGE IN THE EN-TIRE AREA AFFECTED BY THE PRESENCE OF US LOW-COST WORKERS.

BY TAKING TIME OFF FROM SCHOOLWORK TO DEMAND WAGES FOR STUDENTS, WE THINK AND ACT AGAINST THE WORK WE ARE DOING. IT ALSO PUTS US IN A BETTER POSITION TO GET THE MONEY.

NO MORE UNPAID SCHOOLWORK!

THE WAGES FOR STUDENTS STUDENTS

WAGES FOR STUDENTS

Wages for Students, a pamphlet in the form of a blue book, was written and published anonymously by activists linked to the journal *Zerowork* during student strikes in Massachusetts and New York in the fall of 1975. Deeply influenced by the Wages for Housework Campaign's analysis of capitalism and emerging in relation to struggles such as Black Power, anti-colonial resistance, and the antiwar movements, the authors sought to fight against the role of universities as conceived by capital and its state. The pamphlet debates the strategies of the student movement at the time and denounces the regime of forced unpaid work imposed every day upon millions of students. *Wages for Students* was an affront to and a campaign against the neoliberalization of the university, at a time when this process was just beginning. Forty years later, the highly profitable business of education not only continues to exploit the unpaid labor of the students, but now also makes them pay for it. Today, when the student debt situation has us all up to our necks, and when students around the world are refusing to continue this collaboration-ism, we again make this pamphlet available "for education against education."

This new trilingual edition is edited by Jakob Jakobsen, María Berríos, and Malav Kanuga, and includes an introduction by George Caffentzis, Monty Neill, and John Willshire-Carrera. It also includes a transcript of a collective discussion organized by Jakob Jakobsen, Malav Kanuga, Ayreen Anastas, and Rene Gabri, following a public reading of the pamphlet by George Caffentzis, Silvia Federici, Cooper Union students, and other members and friends of 16 Beaver.

THE MENTAL DISCIPLINE FACTORY IN 1965

"It is morning. The Weatherman declares daylight and places the sun (rain, snow, clouds, etc, whichever is most appropriate) in the sky. And like mechanized clock-time, the earth tick-tocks around the sun again."

John Doe belongs to Unit 12 of the Elm City Mental Discipline Factory. He is Our Example for the day. John is Average or was until he Went Wrong. He was sitting in Our physical-need room with his fellow mass-productions, pencil in right hand, paper on table, mind on his own work, busy.

By the way, for some background information. The original excuse for Our physical-need room's existence was for "producing and distributing food to supplement Our disciplinary teachings with physical encouragement and semi-satisfaction." But its purpose now is a gathering place for John Does who aren't scheduled for anything more important. Here we teach them obedience, a very very, very important part of overall mental discipline.

Introduction to the Present Edition

George Caffentzis, Monty Neill,
and John Willshire-Carrera

Wages for Students was published anonymously in the fall of 1975 by three activists. One was an assistant professor at Brooklyn College (part of the City of New York university system) and two were graduate students at University of Massachusetts in Amherst.

It is not surprising that the New York metropolitan area and the state of Massachusetts were the sites of origin of a pamphlet on university student conditions and demands, since both had one of the highest concentrations of tertiary-level students in the United States. New York and Massachusetts were for students what Detroit then was for autoworkers.

Nor was the time of origin surprising in terms of the conjunctures of both theory and history. The authors were all involved with a journal titled *Zerowork*. The journal's theoretical approach was a synthesis of the "workerist" perspective (coming from Italy) and the Wages for Housework Campaign initiated in 1972 by the International Feminist Collective. The

workerist perspective had its roots in the struggles of factory workers in the industrial belt
stretching from Los Angeles through Detroit to
Turin, while Wages for Housework had its roots
in the struggles of unwaged women demanding
a wage for their housework, including the struggle for "welfare rights" in the United States.

By the time *Wages for Students* was written, a theoretical awareness of the fact that "the social" is
a particular type of factory had already emerged.
Through these theoretical conjunctures, the terrain was prepared for the seeds of a new thinking
about students' work as well. Along with these
theoretical and political influences there was the
impact of the change in the role of the universities as conceived by capital and its state.

It had been an axiom of state politics in the
1950s and 1960s that universities served to
increase the productivity of the work force
and social discipline as vehicles for upward
mobility, as well as to sponsor research that
would generate new commodities and methods
of production. Thus, until the late 1960s both
capitalists and workers considered education
a "common good." But in the wake of intense
student struggle in the 1960s—for free speech,
civil rights, women's rights, and against the

draft, the Vietnam war, and the use of universities for military research—there was a decisive change in the capitalist class' attitude to university education.

The nation-wide student strike against the U.S. invasion of Cambodia and the killings of students by soldiers and police at Kent State and Jackson State in 1970 marked a decisive turning point in this respect. The new capitalist consensus was that, instead of producing a reliable and skillful labor force for factories, offices, and the military, the U.S. universities (so recently "cleansed" of leftist professors in the McCarthyist purges of the 1950s and early 1960s) were spawning masses of anti-imperialist and anticapitalist graduates. Absurdly, these rebels were subsidized by state and federal taxes levied in part on corporations. This had to stop. By the 1970s, state authorities and corporations were demanding that "conflict-ridden" campuses be defunded and students be forced to pay for their own education—which was no longer hailed as a common good.

At the time, we did not know how to name the change, but we were aware of a shift to what would soon be called the "neoliberal" university, where education becomes a commodity a student buys, an investment she makes in her future, and the institution itself is modeled on a corporation.

This neoliberalization of the university was just beginning in 1975. *Wages for Students* described and satirized this shift.

At the time of the pamphlet's writing, the authors were also participants in the change that was taking place in the student movement. After being engaged for years with "political issues," like racism in university admissions policy or military recruitment on campus, by the late 1970s students were becoming concerned with "economistic issues."

Demonstrations protesting the defunding of universities, the increase of tuition fees, and the reduction of student aid (scholarships and grants) became commonplace on campuses. In retrospect, we see that this new student mobilization was trying to stop the neoliberalization of the U.S. university system. *Wages for Students* offered a language, a vocabulary to this new student movement. Instead of describing students as consumers or micro-entrepreneurs, investing in their future, it called them workers. Against the escalation of tuition fees, it called for "wages for schoolwork."

Wages for Students was not only a "think piece" or an act of intellectual provocation, though surely it was both. With comrades in the *Zerowork* circle, among others, Wages for Students activists proselytized in universities throughout the Northeast.

The first stage of this political work was to bring the Wages for Schoolwork perspective to students' attention. We launched the idea in Left conferences and student meetings. We wrote fliers, distributed bumper stickers, participated in campus demonstrations, and presented in the classrooms of sympathetic professors. We rejected devising schemes to determine "how much" and "to whom" these wages should be paid. The goal was to create Wages for Students chapters in the universities and build a network that would, for a start, change the discourse of the Left (which was in places hostile to the demand) and what remained of the student movement.

The Wages for Students Campaign took its model from the work of the Wages for Housework Campaign in the U.S., that by the mid 1970s was reaching its organizational zenith. Much of its political organizing was directed against the attack on women on welfare, at the time justified in the name of the "fiscal crisis." The Campaign called "welfare" the first "wages for housework."

Wages for Students learned from this expansion of the wage and sought to apply it to students. Just as the Wages for Housework Campaign saw "welfare benefits" as the first form of wages for housework, Wages for Students activists saw the many forms of student financial aid as first forms of wages for students. We joined demonstrations and organized protests against the cuts to this "aid" which they depicted as a "wage." This campaign, in some places, brought together diverse sectors of the working class, from welfare mothers and community activists to graduate students, many of whom gained access to the university through the civil rights struggles of this period. We understood that although wages for schoolwork, like many other struggles for higher wages, was not in itself a revolutionary demand, putting an end to unwaged labor in all its forms would destabilize, indeed terminate, the capitalist system since so much surplus value is generated by it.

As organizers, we also understood that getting paid a wage for schoolwork would provide us with additional power to alternatively refuse more of the other daily work imposed on us by capital, including the work required to "afford" being put to work in school. Work that denied us time to think, create, share, and care for one another. Like those organizing for wages for housework, we understood that getting paid for schoolwork would ultimately give students greater power to refuse the work imposed on them by capital.

It is clear, in retrospect, that U.S. capital and its state understood that the expansion and inclusivity of the wage that Wages for Housework and Wages for Students promoted was a political threat to the system. It is no accident that many of the neoliberal reforms of the last thirty years have been attacks on welfare rights and free access to university education; and that these attacks have been carried through by both Democrats and Republicans, along with cuts to the wages and benefits of the employed.

Wages for Students, as a demand, came at an ill-starred time when capital's strategists in the U.S. were abandoning the Keynesian policy of subsuming wage struggles to capital's development plans. Thus, instead of wages for students, we have had a tremendous increase in tuition fees (500% between 1985 and the present). The result is that today the average student debtor has a loan debt of nearly $30,000, and the total student loan debt is more than $1.1 trillion. Instead of obtaining wages for students, students in the U.S. have been paying to work at universities and to train themselves for future exploitation.

It is, of course, gratifying to see, forty years after its publication, a renewed interest in what might appear a countercurrent footnote to the neoliberal reform of the university. Of what use can this pamphlet be now for a student movement that is again on the move from Chile to Quebec and many U.S. cities in between? The movements themselves must decide. How this new generation of students will respond to the pamphlet will provide useful political knowledge for us all.

Already we can see, however, that *Wages for Students* can serve at least one purpose. By showing that students are workers and what they do in the universities is not "consuming" a commodity called "higher education," the pamphlet empowers the struggle against student debt. It establishes that it is not the students who owe to the universities, the government, and the banks a huge amount of money. It is these institutions that should be paying students as they—and more importantly capital—thrive on unpaid student labor. In the current period, when politicians are proposing neoliberal "solutions" to the crisis created by student debt, such as ranking universities so as to make students "better shoppers in the education market," *Wages for Students* counters that students are workers engaged in unwaged, exploited labor that must be paid.

New York, 2015

Wages for Students
(A pamphlet in the form of a blue book, 1975)

The 'Wages for Students' Students

The Mental Discipline Factory in 1965

"It is morning. The Weatherman declares day-light and places the sun (rain, snow, clouds, etc., whichever is most appropriate) in the sky. And like mechanized clock-time, the earth tick-tocks around the sun again."

John Doe belongs to Unit 12 of the Elm City Mental Discipline Factory. He is Our Example of the day. John is Average, or was until he Went Wrong. He was sitting in Our physical-need room with his fellow mass-productions, pencil in right hand, paper on table, mind on his own work, busy.

By the way, for some background information. The original excuse for Our physical-need room's existence was for "producing and distributing food to supplement Our disciplinary teachings with physical encouragement and semi-satisfaction." But its purpose is now a gathering place for John Does who aren't scheduled for anything more important. Here we teach them obedience, a very, very, very important part of overall mental discipline.

But about John Doe. He was Alright until he discovered the audacity to get up and go right over to Our water fountain and drink two huge gulps of water, completely filling his mouth and quenching his thirst at our expense.

Now, You've all been disciplined to realize that is not the purpose of Our water fountains. You've been programmed to understand they're for disciplinary temptation and have a part in Our Plan only for that purpose. You have to master your thirst, not like John. He is bad, bad, bad, bad. One of Our supervisors had to have him escorted to the medical surgeon who promptly sewed his lips together.

Some of Us think John's punishment was too slight for such a disgraceful show of disobedience. But We do still believe in mercy. Principle is principle but what is principle worth if humanity is ignored.

Study significance for lecture tomorrow.

(Written in school by a high school student)

What is Schoolwork?

Going to school, being a student is work. This work is called schoolwork although it is not usually considered to really <u>be</u> work since we don't receive any wages for doing it. This does not mean that schoolwork is not work, but rather that they have taught us to believe that only if you are paid do you <u>really</u> work.

Schoolwork takes the form of many different tasks of varying intensities and combinations of skilled and unskilled labor. For example, we are to learn to sit quietly in classrooms for long periods of time and not cause a disturbance. We are to listen attentively and attempt to memorize what is being said. We are to be obedient to teachers. Occasionally we learn certain technical skills that make us more productive when we work in jobs outside of school that require these skills. Most of the time, however, we do a lot of unskilled labor.

The characteristic common to all the specific tasks that schoolwork involves is Discipline, i.e. forced work. Sometimes we are disciplined, which means that we are forced to work by others (teachers, principals, and guards). At other times we are self-disciplined, which means that we force ourselves to do schoolwork. Not surprisingly, the different categories of schoolwork used to be called Disciplines.

Obviously, it is cheaper and better for Capital if we do our own disciplining. This saves paying for more teachers, principals, and guards who are waged workers and have to be paid something. As self-disciplined students, we perform the double task of doing schoolwork and making ourselves do it. That is why school administrators place so much emphasis on the self-disciplinary aspects of school while trying to keep the costs of disciplining us to a minimum.

Like all capitalistic institutions, schools are factories. Grading and tracking are ways of measuring our productivity within the school-factory. Not only are we trained to take our future "position in society" but we are also being programmed to go to our "proper place." The school-factory is an essential step in the selection process that will send some to sweep the streets and some to supervise the sweepers.

Schoolwork may also include some learning that the students themselves find useful. This aspect, however, is rigidly subordinated to Capital's most immediate self-interest: working class discipline. After all, what good to capital is an engineer who speaks Chinese and can solve differential equations if he never shows up for work?

Why Schoolwork?

Most economists agree: "Schoolwork is both a consumption and investment good." So their answer to the question of "why schoolwork?" is that the schooling you get has this marvelous two-sided good about it. Not only do you invest in yourself in such a way that you can expect to get a high paying job in the future but also it is fun! This is a far cry from the days when investment was abstention, but can we take this stuff seriously?

Let us consider the "consumption" side. Since by "consumption good" the economists mean something that is enjoyable, pleasurable and satisfying, then anyone calling schooling a consumption good must be kidding. The constant pressure to finish assignments, the hassle of schedules, the stupid sleepless nights to study for exams, and the rest of the self-disciplining that goes on immediately quells any possible fun. It is like saying that going to prison is a consumption good because it is a pleasure to get out!

Surely one might say that there is some enjoyment going on in school, but it isn't education. Rather, it is <u>the struggle against that education</u> that's enjoyable. It is the trips you take to get away from classes, the love affairs that are so distracting, the meandering conversations in bars, the demonstrations that shut it down, the wrong books read and the right books read at the wrong time; all that you do not to be educated. So on the consumption side, the conclusion is exactly the opposite of the economists.

What about the "investment" side? All throughout the sixties economics professors, bankers, "guidance" counselors agreed: school was a good personal investment. The idea was that you should treat yourself like a little corporation, a mini-GM, so that you could invest in yourself by going to school in the same way a corporation buys machines in order to make a bigger profit operating on the principle: you have to spend money (invest) to make money. If you could raise the money (and the stomach) to go to school either by getting a loan, or working a second job, or getting your parents to pay, you could expect to make a profit on that money because you could expect to get a higher paying job in the future due to your increased schooling. In the heyday of what they called "the human capital revolution," learned economists figured that you would get a better return in investing in your education than if you bought GM stock. This was capitalism for the working class with a vengeance!

Aside from the distaste that this "investment view" might cause—for if you are a corporation then one part of you is going to be a worker and another part of you is going to be the boss over that worker—one might wonder whether you actually get more money from going to school in the long run. In the sixties everyone assured you that you would, but in the "crisis-ridden" seventies all bets are off. The authorities are now saying that their previous analyses were all misconceived, that you cannot expect any such "good return" to your investment in yourself. Not surprisingly it now turns out that you are not a better profit making operation than GM. At best all they can come up with is a possible increase in what they called your "psychic" income, in that if you get more schooling you might land a "nicer" if not a higher paying job; but even this is not guaranteed, especially since all the "nice," "clean" jobs are becoming uncertain, harder to do, and even dangerous, e.g. teaching. It seems that students have been misplanned.

It is obvious to every student that this "investment good" attempt to make you see the wisdom of working for free or even paying to work in school is a phoney. So it is getting harder and harder to convince anyone to shell out money for schooling on the basis of the fairy tale of you as profit-making corporation. So now both sides of the economists' claim collapse, but in the midst of this debacle schoolwork gets a new defender from what might seem to be a surprising quarter: the Left.

The "socialist" teacher and the "revolutionary" student have become the staunchest defenders of the public university against "budget cut-backs" and the like. Why? Their story goes something like this: education leads to the ability to make more and broader connections in your social situation, in a word, education makes you more conscious. Since the public universities open up the possibility of having a highly educated working class, these universities make it possible for the working class to become more class conscious; further, a more conscious working class will pay less attention to the merely "economistic" demands for more money and less work, and pay more attention to the political task of "building socialism." This logic gives the Left both an explanation of the university crisis—capital is afraid of the highly conscious working class that the university was beginning to spawn—and a demand: more schoolwork and not less! So in the name of political consciousness and socialism these leftists intensify schoolwork (which is just wageless work) and frown upon student demands for less of it as capitalistic backsliding. At a time when all the usual defenses of the free work done at schools are being exposed, the Left now seizes the time as its chance to lead the working class out if its "materialistic" sleep to its higher mission: the making of socialistic society.

But the Left runs afoul of that old question posed to previous enlighteners of the working class: who shall educate the educators? Since the Left does not start from the obvious—schoolwork is unwaged work—all its efforts lead to more unwaged work for capital, to more exploitation. All its attempts to increase class consciousness remain oblivious to capital's control on its own ground, and so the Left ends in consistently supporting capital's efforts to intensify work, in rationalizing and disciplining the working class. So the "building of socialism" becomes just another device for getting more free work in the service of capital.

So capital's and the Left's defense of the wageless character of schoolwork just falls on its face.

Students are Unpaid Workers

Students belong to the working class. More specifically, we belong to that part of the working class that is unwaged (unpaid). Our wagelessness condemns us to lives of poverty, dependence, and overwork. But worst of all, not getting a wage means that we lack the power that the wage provides in dealing with capital.

Without the wage we are condemned to lives of bare existence. We are forced to survive on what others wouldn't tolerate. The housing we can afford to rent is substandard and overcrowded. The food we eat, must eat, is cheap institutional food of the cheapest brands. Our clothing and entertainment are standardized and drab. We are a clear case of poverty.

Since we are mostly unwaged and since we do have to live, we have to get the money from somewhere else, by being dependent on someone who does receive a wage. For some students, subsistence and tuition are at least partially taken care of by a dear relative. As unwaged students, however, we are in a relationship of dependence upon our parents or other benefactors that leaves us <u>powerless</u>. Further, if a whole family sacrifices—the mother gets a second job and the father sweats to pay for our schooling, our parents are weakened in their struggle against work while we are blackmailed into accepting the school work. Even though we do as much work as the waged, we are made to be dependent upon them; for with the exception of those students who do receive wages (in the Armed Forces, in the "enlightened" Lompoc Jail in California, in private corporation training programs, in Manpower Training) most students get no wage at all for the schoolwork they do.

For those of us who do not receive such support, not getting a wage means having to work an additional job outside of school. And since the labor market is saturated with students looking for these jobs, capital imposes minimum wages and benefits on us. As a result, we work even more hours or even additional jobs. Since our schoolwork is unpaid, most of us work during the so-called summer vacation. Even if we take the time off we have no money with which to enjoy it. The absurdity of this is even further magnified by the very high productivity requirements which are constantly being imposed on us as students (exams, quizzes, papers, etc.) and by the way we are being programmed so that we impose further productivity requirements on ourselves (extra credit work, outside reading and thinking for our classes—not for ourselves, on-the-job training, student teaching, etc.) On the one hand, we are forced to work for nothing and on the other, we are forced to work for almost nothing.

Of course, we are told that it will all be made up to us in the future. They say that we will be given this meaningful, high-paying job with a secretary. Our free work will not be in vain. But, as we know even before we joyfully dance out of this factory, there is nothing to look forward to but a very depressing job as hotel clerk in the local Holiday Inn, or, at best, as a secretary at our old workplace within the university. The reality of the situation is one in which today students are already starting to get paid for schoolwork:

- Armed Forces; the ROTC pays $100 a month plus tuition for studying
- Some corporations pay their employees to attend night school or continue studying towards advanced degrees
- Jailors at the Lompoc Jail are paying some of their prisoners to do schoolwork at the University of California
- Social Security Benefits
- Scholarship recipients (BEOG)
- Vietnam Era veterans

Wages for Students

We are fed up with working for free.

We demand real money now for the school-work we do.

We must force capital, which profits from our work, to pay for our schoolwork. Only then can we stop depending on financial aid, our parents, working second and third jobs, or working during summer vacations for our existence. We already earn a wage; now we must be paid it. Only in this way can we seize more power to use in our dealings with capital.

We can do a lot with the money. First, we will have to work less as the "need to work" additional jobs disappears. Second, we will immediately enjoy a higher standard of living since we will have more to spend when we take time off from schoolwork. Third, we will raise the average wage in the entire area affected by the presence of us low-cost workers.

By taking time off from schoolwork to demand wages for students, we think and act against the work we are doing. It also puts us in a better position to get the money.

NO MORE UNPAID SCHOOLWORK!

The 'Wages for Students' Students

Wages for Debts, Students for Borrowers, Life for . . .*

16 Beaver, New York
Sunday March 3rd, 2013

Rene Gabri: We thought of a simple format for tonight. The idea is to have Jakob Jakobsen say something about himself and the work that he has been interested in for some time, basically ever since we've known him, around ten years or so, a little more; what brought him to the *Wages for Student*s pamphlet, some questions that he has about it; and maybe then George Caffentzis and Silvia Federici can talk a little bit and try and answer a few of those questions; and then we can all reflect further and bring in our own questions.

---

* This is a a transcription of a conversation that took place in 16 Beaver on Sunday March 3rd, 2013 at 8pm. The discussion lasted two hours and twenty minutes and has been edited due to length. Some repetitive or sidetracking comments have been omitted, but most things said are here, intact.

The discussion was recorded with the consent of all present and the editors have tried to contact all those whose interventions are transcribed here. Nevertheless, as the meeting was a public event it has not been possible to identify all speakers, thus the appearance in the transcription of eight "unidentified participants."

Jakob Jakobsen: Thank you. We have actually been discussing the structure of this meeting quite a lot, though also quite loosely. And we all disagree, which is a good point of departure for a discussion. So I hope this is going to be a conversational evening more than a presentation. And hopefully people will ask and talk as they feel like it . . .

RG: And interrupt.

JJ: The reason I think we are meeting tonight is this booklet, *Wages for Students*, which I found in the Anarchist Bookfair in London a couple of years ago. Because I know Silvia and George, I wrote Silvia and asked whether they knew anything about this, and Silvia said "Yes, of course, that's George." The reason I asked was because *Wages for Students* connects to Silvia's work in Wages for Housework, so I had some idea that Silvia might know. The reason I picked this pamphlet up was—to say a little bit about myself, but not too much—because I have been researching in educational histories or educational struggles for a while. And I have been working in producing an archive for a research project on the Antiuniversity of London, an experimental university born in 1968, that lasted for about three years—it's not really clear when it actually stopped, which reveals a little about its experimental structure. It was self-organized and run by the students. This also caused this anti-institution to be slowly deinstitutionalized and disappear into the social fabric of London and the world. The reason I think it is important to talk about these things is to connect struggles in time—the *Wages for Students* pamphlet is from 1975—and also to connect struggles in terms of space. I've been living in London and following the struggles in education over there, and I was very interested in coming here and talking with George and Silvia, and all of you, and hear about what is going on here in New York. So I was hoping very much that I was coming here to listen and not to talk. What I would suggest now, unless you have other plans, is that we read this pamphlet together.

Malav Kanuga: Will we take turns?

JJ: Yes.

[*Collective reading of* Wages for Students *pamphlet*]

JJ: I will come back to you George, but I would like to start with a question for you, Silvia. This understanding of study-work as labor within the framework of the capitalist economy, as unpaid labor, is—at least for me—an interesting idea to consider. And, of course, this is linking to the struggles and all the work you have been doing on the relation between productive and reproductive labor. Where the productive labor is the labor in the factory that is acknowledged and connected to a wage, while the reproductive labor is the work somehow underpinning the productive labor, as housework and student work, and so on. The interesting question is the relationship between the productive and the reproductive labor, both in terms of the housework, but also in terms of the student work. So I would like to ask you, Silvia, if you could reflect on this conception of student work as unpaid labor within capitalist production.

Silvia Federici: It was a logical consequence of conceptualizing domestic labor as part of the broader range of activities by which labor-power is produced. It was realizing that there is an assembly line that runs not only through the factories, but through the whole of society— the homes, the schools—producing workers, who then produce commodities and profit. Redefining housework as work that produces labor-power provided a new perspective on the function of schooling. The school is a continuation of the home; it trains and disciplines future workers. Disciplining new generations is also an important aspect of housework. This is what makes it so difficult. It's not only the physical work, but the fact that it involves a constant struggle, having to say "no," and "you cannot do this." Self-discipline may be necessary independent of the capitalist organization of work; but in most cases the discipline we teach our children is dictated by our expectations of what will happen to them once they enter the labor market. It is the mothers' and the fathers' work to shape our desire, to make sure that we fit with the expectations of the labor market.

It was very important for women, and for the feminist movement, to realize this because there was always a tremendous guilt associated to the idea of struggling against housework. Refusal of housework carried so much guilt because women felt they were undermining the wellbeing of their families, the wellbeing of the people they were supposed to care for. So being able to identify and disentangle those aspects of housework that are specifically demanded by the production of a worker, the production of a person who is destined to be exploited, was a liberating process. We began to realize that we could either reproduce people for the struggle or we could reproduce them for the labor market. Of course, the line is not always so clear. But it was liberating because it made it possible to think that the struggle against housework does not have to be a struggle against people we care for.

That thinking was carried over into our approach to schoolwork. A great part of our schoolwork, whether we study French or Mathematics, is learning to be disciplined. This is the first thing we are expected to learn. Wages for Housework enabled us to see that schools prepare us to work for our future employers and that we mostly go to school because we need a certificate, not for the pleasure of studying. It enabled us to see that how a school is organized is dictated by the needs of the labor market. It also gave us insights into the consequences of students' economic dependence. If you don't earn a wage, then you depend on those who pay your way, and in that dependence there is an unequal power relation. Some people say: "If your husband earns a wage, then you too have some money." But you don't. Whatever money you are given, you have to be grateful for it. It is not something that you are entitled to. It is the same with students. When you earn a wage through your work then you have some autonomy, at least from family and community. But if you work for nothing, then you must depend on other people. Moreover, when you are socially defined as unwaged workers, as students and houseworkers are, then you are also destined to become cheap labor and any time you get a job you are paid less than other workers. There is a close connection between the condition of the houseworker and the condition of the student. Clearly, the people from the Zerowork collective who wrote *Wages for Students* were inspired by Wages for Housework.

George Caffentzis: Yes.

SF: It is also amazing to see how current the pamphlet still is. Particularly in the first part, you see that we were already confronting a neoliberal ideology. Already in the 1970s you had the beginning of the neoliberal idea of education as a self-investment, though they could not fully implement it until they dismantled the welfare state, the investment of the state in education and other forms of reproduction.

JJ: This was written . . .

SF: . . . in 1975, years before the full blossoming of neoliberalism, but in a context where the writing was on the wall. Especially in New York, they were beginning to tell us: "We don't owe you an education, you should pay for it."

JJ: Maybe people here know more, but I understand it was in 1976 that CUNY (City University of New York) became fee based. In 1975, when this was published, it was actually a free university—free in money terms. But George, what especially caught my attention in the text was the "education against education" perspective. Today there are lots of struggles going on inside the universities against cutbacks and against privatization, and for the preservation of the institution. But here you are criticizing the Left for clinging to an institutional model that is basically disciplinarian, a model that is forming, shaping, and molding students to become obedient laborers. Here there is this—what you could call—more "anarchic" current, I haven't seen a lot in the present. People tend to cling to their disciplining institutions, instead of leaving them or challenging them radically. There is not much self-organizing outside the institutions using "education against education" as you were suggesting. Maybe you can tell us more of how this came about?

GC: The text for *Wages for Students* was written in 1975 at the moment when the first issue of *Zerowork* was being put together. It was done by three people: myself and two others, John Willshire-Carrera and Leoncio Schaedel, who were graduate students at the University of Massachusetts in Amherst in the Economics Department. I was still working on my PhD thesis at the time and teaching at Brooklyn College of the City University in New York. We were all involved in a politics that brought together what we thought to be two conceptual and political revolutions. The first was Wages for Housework that opened up the whole universe of unwaged labor. This had a profound effect upon those of us who had grown up in a Marxist framework that saw wage labor as being the foundation of capitalist society, and also the waged working class as foundation of the transition to a society beyond capitalism . . . [*loud garbage truck begins recollection work outside. GC raises his voice while it passes*] This created a whole new way of understanding the nature of work. The second conceptual and political revolution placed [*partly inaudible*] the refusal of work as the basis upon which class struggle operates. From this perspective, class struggle has at its root the rejection of work, not the identification with work. The latter had been for a long period of time one of the mainstays of Marxist and leftist politics, and much of the association with a liberatory notion of education, for example. The pamphlet puts this attitude into question and argues that what's important is how much we *don't* give to capital and how much we reject the identification with being the worker. This was quite basic for the way of operating and thinking in *Wages for Students* . . . Let me touch this thing [*GC reaches for the pamphlet*].

SF: The parallel idea was the Left telling women that getting a job outside is the way to emancipation: "Get a job, join the union, join the class struggle. That is how you gain social power and become part of the working class."

GC: Right. Needless to say, almost forty years later, I have many reflections on this pamphlet. You should realize that the writing, printing, and distributing the pamphlet was part of a political campaign. We started up as a small group of people and we ended up with a small group of people [*laughter*]. But in-between, we did spend a number of years agitating for the demand. We were part of the struggles against the charging of tuition at CUNY in 1976. I myself was very angry with the Professional Staff Congress—the faculty union of CUNY professors—that negotiated with the university around this issue. I had a critique of the actions of the union at the time, and of the Left in general, which viewed the universities as the vehicle by which liberation can occur, as you mentioned Silvia.

They posed the university factory as a place of liberation, whereas we were arguing that it was time to detach ourselves from these factories and begin to say "no" to them.

I have especially thought about this pamphlet recently because of the work my comrades and I have done with the Occupy Student Debt Campaign and Strike Debt. From the vantage point of the present I can see how far we've gone in this struggle. We were fighting for wages for students in the 1970s and now we are trying to escape debt slavery; for the last forty years students have increasingly taken on tremendous debt, literally, in order to be exploited. This development did not happen by accident. Already by the late 1960s and early 1970s capital's strategists, for example Gary Becker, were already working on a blueprint for a neoliberal university before the term "neoliberalism" achieved its present meaning. This is documented in *Wages for Students* and is one of the pamphlet's contributions to the present. What has happened in the last forty years is simply the working out of that neoliberal strategy to its dismal conclusion—and definitely vindicates Thomas Carlyle's curse on economics as a "dismal science." We know the dismal conclusion . . . As I look around this room, I'm sure that I see people who are confronting a dismal future of debt repayments and defaults ad infinitum. This is a type of outcome that we hoped we could stop and even reverse at the time of writing the *Wages for Students* pamphlet. But the forces at work were too strong.

SF: So now you have to pay to be exploited. You have to pay for the privilege of being trained for your future exploitation. It's a double exploitation.

GC: Yeah, it's madness.

JJ: But to continue with this critique of the educational institution as basically a disciplining machine. Instead of following the argument that claims education as a means for working class people to move up class-wise, or as a way of raising consciousness, you didn't see education as a way to liberation. I think your critique of the educational system as such was much more total, you weren't being pragmatic about the possible gains of education.

GC: At this point we were arguing that what was important was the question of power and not of consciousness. We thought that what was crucial was to change the relationships of power, which we thought were rooted in the wage. The argument that we developed in the pamphlet, and moved into the Wages for Students campaign, was that the true transformation of the university would involve an increased capacity for students to organize their own behavior and basically break the work of discipline that was crucial for capitalist education. That was the logic, both implicit and explicit, of the text that was very openly stated. So you are right, in that sense it was a critique of education.

JJ: Also relating it to what is happening today with debt, and debt enslavement, you can also see debt as a disciplining measure.

GC: Oh, double!

SF: And grading! A book should be written about the leftist grading night! The "degrading" night of the leftist teacher. I've had so many conversations with leftist colleagues about it . . .

RG: The degrading night of the leftist?

SF: Yes, the de-grading night of the leftist teacher. Does anyone understand what I am talking about?

Ayreen Anastas: Yes. You have to hand in the grades tomorrow . . .

SF: Yes. Tomorrow you have to grade your students, but you are an enlightened teacher and you know, of course, what grading means. You know that it is the essence of a class system. Nevertheless, you have an idea of education as being so uplifting and so potentially able to inspire you to revolution—you may have been teaching a course on Marx—that you want to make sure the students take seriously what you teach. So you have to decide if it is a B, or a B- or a C+. Maybe even a C-, or a D. People spend nights making these decisions, wanting to be fair to the students and to the course, but generally abstracting from the context in which these decisions are made, which is one that demands that we make a selection, which in most cases has a class basis. This is one of those moments in which the truth comes to the surface. The end of the semester in the course on Marx and Revolution [*laughter*], when students have to be graded. Those who fail it will have to take the class again and pay more money; and if they fail enough classes they will have to go sweep the streets. There are many ways in which we can lose sight of what the university is, of the factory system, the selection machine that it is. The criticism here is not so much that many in the Left—all of us for that matter to the extent we accept to grade—accept this system, but that we pretend we are not contributing to the selection, because presumably we teach consciousness-raising courses. It is interesting for instance that there hasn't been a big struggle in the United States, from students or from teachers, to abolish the grading system. Some radical teachers give all A's, but it is not easy to do it, unless there is a struggle. In Italy, in the 1970s, students were able to impose the group-grade. They couldn't abolish grading, but they imposed group-grading. Basically fifteen, twenty people would take the exam collectively and would receive one grade. Now it is all gone, but for some years it was widely applied.

Unidentified participant 1: Was there other work at that time, amongst the students, that was collaborative?

SF: There was a lot of collaborative work—for example, imposing a certain curriculum—to decide what should be studied. And then there was the struggle for the *pre-salario*, which means the "pre-wage," which is analogous to wages for students.

JJ: This campaign, Wages for Students, was more about the economic side of student life. Unlike the 1960s, which were more about liberation in a wider perspective (sex, gender, race, and many other new ways of understanding repression and liberation), in the 1970s, the struggle again centered around money, capital. Looking at the situation today, much further down the ladder in terms of students' rights and conditions in society, I am wondering: what mystification has capital been able to get away with? It's been a pretty significant operation to move from free education in the mid-1970s to today's situation with student debt enslavement. I'm just wondering what kind of mechanisms are operating here.

GC: The mechanisms by which this happened had to do with, in one sense, the end of the Keynesian relationship between classes that develops in the 1950s and 1960s, and which goes into crisis in the 1970s. What increasingly begins to happen is the transformation—not only in universities for students, but one that takes place all across the board—in the sphere of reproduction. So, for example, what happened with the students in the 1970s is similar to what happened in the end of welfare.

SF: That is very important. The attack on free admission, in the U.S., happened at the same time as the attack on women on welfare started. All the people receiving some assistance from the state, and most of all women receiving AFDC (Aid to Families With Dependent Children), were vilified. This was a program for sole supported mothers, who received some assistance on the assumption that raising children is work, and that "society" benefits from investment in the new generations. But by the 1970s a massive campaign was mounted that denigrated women on welfare as "free riders," "parasites," and "frauds." There was a strong racial element in it, because the women fighting for welfare were mostly black, though the majority of women on welfare were white. It was the beginning of the long road that, in 1996, led to the abolition of the welfare system under Clinton, and increasingly to the vilification of people on Social Security. Today being on Social Security is presented as socially destructive—the elderly are practically accused of bankrupting the country and destroying the future of the new generations, even though Social Security money is money taken from their own paychecks.

GC: The way this took place, had many, many stages. Certainly, the first steps that took place at the university level begins by opening a new way of organizing, for example, the financing of universities that transformed the way they operate, pure and simple, from top to bottom.

They begin to slowly transform themselves into machines that are fed by tuition fees, and to have a very open expression of a corporate structure, even though they present themselves as non-profit, public institutions—even the private universities. In that sense, they begin to create an environment that has a logic of its own. Once you begin to create a situation where the university itself can only operate on the basis of student fees, then there's a logic to it that leads to ever increasing fees. There's a mathematics to it. There is "no way out." So we begin to have a type of university system that leads to the present situation, and which is intensified in the financial and economic crisis. And in order to survive the crisis, university fees continue to rise and create micro-crises by the millions among students and their families.

JJ: George, you have also mentioned, elsewhere, that in the 1960s there was a lot of state money invested in the universities, and what they got in return was rebellion, so in the 1970s the state withdrew from campus. They understood that capital was even better at disciplining than the state was. Money is the best way to discipline people. You could say that was the conclusion of the 1960s.

GC: And it worked in a very important sense. The transformation of the universities is so clear for everyone, it is common knowledge now. Our critique of the life of students is now just common knowledge. The question now is not the critique of it, but what we are going to do about it, because the situation has turned so radically against the power of students to determine their lives.

RG: There's a dimension of both of these struggles—wages for housework and wages for schoolwork—that is really interesting. The demand for wages for a particular kind of labor that is not seen as labor, is a horizon of a kind of struggle that could reshape the field itself. Because, although you say, George, that it's now common knowledge, I'm not so sure what parts of these struggles have entered the common knowledge—I'm sure most of us did not know about this struggle for wages for student work, and I'm wondering what part of these campaigns has potency still. Current struggles tend to be reacting against, for example, the raising of fees. But what would be the horizon of the struggle today? What kind of struggle could reshape the field, or our way of looking at the situation today? Part of the problem seems to be our perception of the situation.

Alan Smart: One thing that comes up in the pamphlet is that in the crisis of the 1970s there weren't these good jobs around anymore. It seems like it is referencing the full implications of the post-industrial condition in the West. Now we see this much more advanced. Now, at least in the rhetoric, not only is welfare perceived as parasitical handouts, but all wages are. The worker who expects to be paid by the hour is perceived as being not enthusiastic enough. Your mention of this new "entrepreneurial" rhetoric, where everyone is not just a little corporation, but you're a "startup," an "artist," a "creative worker." This kind of labor is actually, under the old industrial model, all reproductive; management is reproductive, finance is reproductive. So now what gets suppressed and denied and off-shored, or sent to China, is the actual *production* of things. If the low-end reproductive work is housework that makes you able to keep working, the high-end of that is finance, management, and marketing, which enables the venture to succeed. It seems like the gap between those has been narrowed, so that we are now all entrepreneurs and freelancers working on our laptops, in our underwear, in the bedrooms that we rent and clean up as we work. Anything being produced, and the wages that you get for labor, are impolite things that we can't mention. In the 1990s boom, the idea was that if you were exuberant enough and young enough, you would get funding from Wall Street, you would burn through, succeed, and it was like a gift. You know it wasn't debt, it was like equity, a "risk." Now the exploitation . . .

SF: Now the exploitation is hidden.

AS: I feel a kind of nostalgia for the potential negativity of wages, where a waged worker is not at risk, and even if the people that you work for make much more money off your labor than you do, you know that if they miss their bid, or they mess up, that they still have to pay you. Whereas now everything is entrepreneurial, and you are supposed to make "proposals" in your own time.

SF: And you face your employers alone.

JJ: I was reading about a company where 60% of workers were interns, they had no wage. Then I thought maybe, in ten years interns will have to pay to go to work [*laughter*]. This is the logic of what happened in the university. We are told it is a privilege to go to work, basically. So soon there will be a fee structure, where you can have an amazing job if you pay enough.

SF: It's the universities that are constantly feeding interns to companies. More and more courses today require an internship. In this way the university can extract labor not only directly from the students, but indirectly through the internship system. Companies have been known to lay off their workers, because they get interns from the universities.

RG: It would be nice if there are students here from any of the universities—I mean I know there are because I know some—if they could try and relate some of the questions being raised in this pamphlet to contemporary conditions and struggles.

Unidentified participant 2: A couple of us go to Cooper Union. I actually just finished, and what happened in 1976 at CUNY is happening to us right now. So the question of what would reshape the field, or how to resist it, what kind of powers do we have to oppose tuition . . . The entire community of ex-students and alumni is opposed to the fee structure, but those high up on the boards of trustees are all business people who don't engage with us; they follow a capitalist model, they call it "realistic." That's a really imminent situation for us. So if you have an answer to that question . . . [*Laughter*].

Leo Caione: I want to take advantage of what Rene said. Actually I was a student in Venice, I am Italian, and what I want to say regarding the pamphlet is a change in terms of time. I can give a kind of testimony. I don't want to talk about me, but I will just use my experience as an example. I am anachronistic because I come from a different generation—when I was at school I had to work to go to school. This when I was really young, eleven years old. Now students are really spoiled. I see university students not valuing the things that I valued: the possibility of studying. The pamphlet is almost forty years old and the point of view has really changed. At that time perhaps many things were true, but today, students are spoiled. They don't want to do anything!

Unidentified participant 3: There are probably spoiled people in every generation. I don't think you can make that generalization.

LC: I mean, there are professionals today who—in order to get their education—had to make sacrifices that we have no idea about.

Unidentified participant 4: There is also a shift, to sidestep this more moralistic point, the space of education has become transactional. It is one where students feel "entitled" because they are paying money for a class. So something has happened to the educational space in light of that.

SF: I'm sorry but I have been in the school system in this country for forty years and what you say is not my experience. The students I taught did a lot of work and made sacrifices. They were not "spoiled." When someone has three jobs, in addition to going to school, to pay for tuitions and other costs, they are making sacrifices.

Unidentified participant 5: I think it's really fascinating how it has come to be that, whether students are having a free education or they are paying $50,000 a year in the New School, they are always somehow characterized as "spoiled" by some parts of society. It's a fascinating thing how this can be the case whether you are working three jobs, you are thousands of dollars in debt, or whether you are "enjoying" a free education. We used to have a kind of principle that there was a *right* to education, and that indeed a society owes its younger generation something like this. It's possible to have the experience of "spoiled" students, but this is a discourse that really just works to exacerbate the possibility of a shared analysis of exploitation across groups, like students or the working class.

I had never heard the proposition Wages for Students. I come from the U.K. where there are actually still on-going university occupations here and there. Even now, though the wave of student demonstrations was about two years ago, the struggle continues. I think it is exactly the right thing to do at a point when people are increasingly using this populist line of attack where somehow it's portrayed as a privilege to get into this situation of discipline and debt. Precisely when people are saying, "well if you want to go down this route, now you need to pay £9,000 a year tuition . . ." This is decadence. Even right-wing journalists are saying that it is not an investment anymore to have a degree. It's a fantastic response, just at the point where they are beginning to charge us three times the amount of tuition, to say "we will demand wages, instead, for this work." I think it is a really exciting political proposition. I'm really glad that I heard it being read out in this way. It must have been a wonderful thing hearing your pamphlet read out like that [*laughter*].

GC: I assure you when we wrote it over the kitchen table in those years we had no idea it would be a subject of interest decades later. Anyway, there are parts of this story of what happened between 1975 and 2013 that need to be reflected upon. I am not sure that it has been told yet or even thought through. But it's worth doing.

Unidentified participant 6: I feel that there is something missing from the discussion: the question of "What do we do?" Can we reexamine the value of education from the side of the worker rather than from the side of the capitalist? I think that it is important to understand the difference between the labor process and the learning process, and to try and make a distinction between those things. Also in relation to this idea of students being spoiled, or the manner in which the nature of education itself has changed over the last forty years, and how the educational commodity is consumed in a different manner than it was then. The production of that commodity itself dictates how it's consumed by the student. It seems to me that to demand wages is not necessarily a good thing. Still you are getting exploited when you are receiving wages.

RG: Partly those questions are addressed in the text that Silvia wrote in 1974, "Wages against Housework." She talks clearly about how the wage is not the object of the struggle. Talking about wages is also about opening up that field and understanding those relations very differently. So there is this question about learning versus labor. In a way, because of this intermittency of work today, part of the way capitalism functions, you are constantly having to reshape what you know and how you know between the times that you are remunerated, so that learning is embedded in the process of the market place and adapting to it. Maybe somebody here is already preparing to pitch their new course and is picking up ideas. You never know what will secure you that next job, or gig, or whatever it is. It is ever more difficult to separate the place of learning from labor, as more and more of the labor in these overdeveloped parts of the world require a certain kind of knowledge, which is changing and adapting to everchanging circumstance.

JJ: I think what George is pointing to, is that knowledge is actually discipline, and the whole thing about "spoiled students" relates to the fact that students have a lot of power inside the universities because they are now consumers. Courses are not run if there are not ten students signing up for them. The power hierarchy inside the universities has changed. From a neoliberal point of view it is student centered, but you could also say that this is working as a disciplining tool, where students are basically shaped as consumers, and they are acting as consumers because they are paying for their studies. Learning is in this context more like neoliberal disciplining, as far as I see it—students here have to correct me now. This change of the understanding of the student, in terms of "I am paying this much, I can demand these things" is also structuring the university today.

Alexander Dwinell: Also related to this idea of "self-investment," it seems the only reason for education is to prepare yourself to be able to work. But I don't feel that a lot of the skills you learn in university have any direct relation to what you do in a given job. And yet you can't get that job without making that physical sacrifice or indebting yourself. More and more, it seems to be the only reason people talk about the value of education. That puts blinders on our ability to talk about the real value of education. Even with Cooper Union, it's like "we have to charge for tuition because the financial market has changed and now we can't provide it." Without ever getting into any of the reasons why there ever was free access to education.

Unidentified participant 7: It's funny how the word "spoiled" gets thrown around. In the

Quebec struggle *that* was the main media attack on the student movement: that these were "spoiled children." It is interesting, because, what is a spoiled child? A spoiled child is an undisciplined child, who doesn't do what they are told, right? That's where the word comes from, and then it gets imported into talking about post-secondary students. I have taught lots of students who sit in the back and go "oh no, he's talking about Marx *again*." It is very tempting to think of them as spoiled students, but I started thinking about it and talking to them, and they are buying an education. They are buying a credential. Most of the students I have talked to have a very nascent sense that the critical elements of the curriculum were actually going to impede their ability to perform, more than help them. So what if that "laziness" or "undisciplinedness" is actually a form of inchoate resistance that has to be organized. What if it is about saying "Frankly, the society that I am going to graduate into doesn't give a fuck about me, so why would I bother? What do I owe these people? Why would I work hard in this? Why would I want to take advantage of it?" It's very tempting to think we should be organizing with the gung-ho students who are really into school and learning. But I think that the vast majority of students in the system right now—who are not spoiled but incredibly disciplined and exploited—should be worked with. The problem is not that students aren't disciplined enough; it's that they are not angry enough.

RG: I think we are missing one part of the picture, which is, from what Leo's saying, a class dimension. It's easy to dismiss this idea of the "spoiled student," but even in my own perception, coming from a poorer, immigrant circumstance, my first experience of college was exactly "I am with a lot of spoiled kids." I felt a tremendous weight as in "people are suffering really shitty lives so that I can be in this school supposedly to have a better life." Those conditions really shape the way you perceive the people around you; I can understand how you can be in that position and see others as antagonistic or somehow outside a certain principle of reality. We can talk around it, by saying that students are incredibly hardworking, or what we perceive as spoiledness is something that is a kind of resistance. Both of those things are actually true and I don't disagree, but nevertheless there is a split within classes, in the sense that those coming from more affluent backgrounds and those coming from more working class backgrounds, or immigrant conditions, perceive what it is to be in college in very different ways—it is not a given. So it is easy for those people who see affluent people occupying a hall to be dismissive and say "they can do that because they have rich parents, and at the end of the day I've got to get a job, and I have a mountain of shit to deal with, bills and debt." This is also what we are struggling against. We can't just talk our way around that division, but have to find a way to address it. And it can be complicated when you have experiences of severe impoverishment from another place and come here and think "this is a great place, there is a lot more opportunity compared to where I came from." I disagree with the judgment that all students are spoiled, but we have to acknowledge that class is a major problem.

LC: I don't want to be misunderstood in relation to what I said about spoiled students. I know there are people, like me, who had to work three jobs to be in university.

AA: But the discussion is about the bigger situation. You said "I don't want to put myself at the center." It is important to get out of your experience, it is important to move on from your experience. Also to think with others: "Who are the others I can think with? How can I change this situation?"

GC: In the forty years between this pamphlet's first publication and today, I have seen with my own eyes and felt on my skin, the defeat of this pamphlet's politics and the consequences of that defeat. It took me quite a while to understand the deep consequences for my students. By the late 1990s and early years of this century, what begins to happen is that my students, who are at a proletarian university in Maine, increasingly, not only have to pay for tuition fees that begin to grow much faster than inflation, but also they are beginning to face an eternal indebtedness which was new for them and their families. I was oblivious for many years of this transformation. I didn't see what was happening with my own students. I was like that "good" radical teacher who spent many nights grading whether or not a student understood the notion of the alienation of labor in Marx, without actually recognizing the fact that these students were having to pay off enormous debt, in order for them to be in my class where they could study alienation! Over the last few years I have begun to do penance, I have begun to commit myself to changing this. Whatever I can do I have been trying to do—with some comrades I see here— in the Occupy Student Debt campaign, and in other efforts like Strike Debt, to bring this out. I'm talking about a generalized condition for the large majority of students: in order to go into a university they are increasingly going to be indebted. These are consequences, as far as I see, that have a tremendously disarming effect. If the current struggles against student debt and for free access to university education do not succeed, a whole generation will not be able to organize an autonomous type of struggle against capital. One of the first steps of changing this outcome is to change the relationship of student loan debtors and the forces that have them in their claws. In this discussion it seems vital that before we can begin to demand wages for students we have to get rid of the debts that students are facing at this point.

JJ: Some of the ethos in your pamphlet is against education. I am in a way puzzled by the fact that so many students—all of us in a way—go with open eyes into university, this disciplining factory, knowing what is going to happen.

GC: The point was that we wanted to transform alienation into a power. In other words, instead of alienation being a condition of defeat, what we were trying to do—through the transforming of the process of being in a university into a wage relation—was on the one side, to recognize schoolwork as exploitation, and on the other for the student to recognize his or her alienation from it. In that sense, yes, *Wages for Students* is against education. But there is another irony in this, because it's exactly in that alienation process that you learn what is the struggle and you can begin to struggle. There's a twist upon a twist here.

JJ: Struggle *is* school. Education is struggle, not obedience.

GC: Exactly . . . Similar things are also at work in reproductive labor in the house.

JJ: Our friends from Cooper Union, I'm just wondering, are you discussing leaving school, or saying "fuck school"? Or organizing the students and making your own school?

Unidentified participant 8: That's kind of where my mind goes, but we actually haven't imagined possible futures.

Victoria Sobel: I come from a similar background and attend a tuition free university. I come from one half first-generation immigrants, the other half second-generation immigrants. I think a class analysis of what is happening is crucial. There are two things at play. There is the stratification of those who can afford to go to school and sit and be there. And those who are becoming increasingly indebted by going into school. Talking about the student struggle, I agree that whether you enter the collegial space or not has to do with class and access. It's interesting what you were saying about the privileged students occupying the halls. In my case, and in many of my peers' case, it was actually the opposite. I was perhaps one of the more marginalized and indebted students. I'm not in a place where I can allow this to go any further. You see both sides: the most indebted students, and those who have the space, and have always had the space, stand up. It is either a question of how to merge those and reclaim space, which is what I think we are trying to do at our school, or maybe, start something new.

Graeme Thomson: If education is becoming a commodity with increasingly diminished returns against indebtedness, in the framework of the institution, it begs the question: shouldn't education move outside the institution? At least in terms of what we value education for. It seems that one is going almost suicidally into this question of indebtedness. Particularly as more and more we ask, what is the value of having a degree? It's not getting you anywhere and the horizon of emancipation is no longer there. So why are people still equating education with the university if more and more the value isn't there?

SF: In many cases it is desperation, because you cannot get a job unless you have a certain certificate. Though you have few chances of getting a job with it, you know that this is what you must do. You don't have much choice. That is why people keep wanting the certificate and pay for it, hoping it will give them some security.

AD: Also I think there's the factor of private colleges within this struggle. I don't think we've talked enough about them in this discussion. That's where a significant part of student debt is being incurred, for even less valuable degrees in a lot of instances. It's really like the mortgage foreclosure, as in: "Ok. We are extending credit for a brief period of time to get you totally sucked into this system and then we are going to steal everything from you, but you will still have to pay us back." It is totally trapping people and eliminating the possibility of thinking of anything other than survival on a day-to-day basis.

Themis Pellas: I don't know if any of you were in the student union that had some meetings last semester, but we discussed how we can go beyond a student union, and have a workers' union that is city wide. Which means you have to understand that students and workers move between this bridge, and not forget that what universities are doing is preparing the professions that are going to be outside. So you have to work on both edges, and also in-between. How do you intervene in this complex situation? By intervening in all these positions, I would say. This means that you have to create the professions that you want while you are in the university. There is an interesting thing happening in Occupy because people from different universities are trying to figure out terms of mutuality with other people, "how am I valuable to them?" If I want to go beyond the institutions, I have to reconfigure myself. We need to have these wider struggles.

SF: It helps to make the parallel between education and healthcare because you can make the same argument. You can say: "There are a lot of rich people who don't need it, so we shouldn't have universal healthcare." In fact people make this argument all the time. But we could also say: "We should create another healthcare system outside the market." People are trying to create alternatives, because we know that the healthcare we get is not good. Still, we cannot abandon the medical system as it is because we don't have the means to replace it yet. I see the struggle of education and healthcare as part of the same process. There are different ways in which we can begin to change them. If we see them as frozen, we are lost. Students are not alone, we have to see their struggle in a broader context. Otherwise we cannot go beyond the particular tactics and this is a defeat.

JJ: Just one last thing about self-organized education. We had the Copenhagen Free University in Denmark and the state made a law outlawing and forbidding us to use the term "university." Capital is scared of students getting ideas about organizing their own universities. Even though we didn't exist at the time—we had closed in 2007—we got this letter telling us that if we ever considered reopening the Copenhagen Free University, it would be illegal. All these small measures are adding up.

SUELDO PARA ESTUDIANTES

Sueldo para Estudiantes, panfleto en la forma de un cuaderno celeste, fue escrito y publicado de manera anónima en el otoño de 1975 por tres activistas vinculados a la revista *Zerowork* durante las huelgas estudiantiles en Massachusetts y Nueva York en el otoño de 1975. Fuertemente influenciado por la campaña Sueldo para el Trabajo Domestico y su análisis del capitalismo, emerge en relación a luchas como el Black Power, la resistencia anticolonial y los movimientos anti-guerra. Los autores deseaban luchar contra la manera en que el capital y su Estado concebía la universidad y el rol que le otorgaba. El panfleto debate las estrategias del movimiento estudiantil de ese entonces y denuncia el régimen de trabajo forzoso no-remunerado impuesto día a día a millones de estudiantes. *Sueldo para Estudiantes* fue una afronta y una campaña contra la neoliberalización de la universidad, cuando este proceso apenas comenzaba. Cuarenta años después, la empresa altamente lucrativa de la educación no solo continúa aprovechándose del trabajo impago de los estudiantes, sino que encima cobra por ello. Hoy, cuando la situación de deuda estudiantil nos tiene a todos hasta el cuello, y cuando los estudiantes del mundo entero se están rehusando a continuar colaborando, ponemos nuevamente a disposición este panfleto "por la educación, contra la educación".

Nueva edición al cuidado de Jakob Jakobsen, María Berríos y Malav Kanuga, con introducción de George Caffentzis, Monty Neill, y John Willshire-Carrera. Incluyendo la transcripción de una discusión post-lectura colectiva del panfleto entre George Caffentzis, Silvia Federici, Jakob Jakobsen, Malav Kanuga, Ayreen Anastas, Rene Gabri, estudiantes de Cooper Union y otros miembros y amigos de 16 Beaver.

LA FÁBRICA DE DISCIPLINA MENTAL EN 1965

"Es de mañana. El señor del tiempo anuncia el alba e instala el sol (la lluvia, la nieve, las nubes, etcétera, lo que sea más apropiado) en el cielo. Y como un reloj mecánico la tierra hace tic-tac alrededor del sol una vez más."

Fulano pertenece a la Unidad 12 de la Fábrica de Disciplina Mental de Elm City. Es Nuestro Ejemplo del día. Fulano es una persona común y corriente, o lo era hasta que falló. Estaba sentado en Nuestra sala de necesidades físicas junto a otros productos en masa, sus colegas, con un lápiz en la mano derecha, un papel sobre la mesa, la mente puesta en su trabajo, ocupado.

A propósito, algunos antecedentes. El pretexto original para la existencia de Nuestra sala de necesidades físicas fue "producir y distribuir comida que supla Nuestras instrucciones disciplinarias con estímulo físico y semi-satisfacción". Pero su propósito ahora es servir como lugar de reunión para Fulanos, Sutanos y Menganos que no estén designados a nada más importante. Acá les enseñamos obediencia, una parte muy, pero muy importante de la disciplina mental total.

Introducción a la presente edición

George Caffentzis, Monty Neill,
y John Willshire-Carrera

Sueldo para Estudiantes fue escrito y publicado de manera anónima en el otoño de 1975 por tres activistas. Uno era profesor asistente en el Brooklyn College (parte del sistema de la City of New York University) y los otros dos eran estudiantes de posgrado en la Universidad de Massachusetts en Amherst.

No es sorprendente que el área metropolitana de Nueva York y el estado de Massachussets fueran los lugares en que surgió un panfleto sobre las condiciones y demandas de los estudiantes universitarios, dado que la concentración de estudiantes de nivel terciario en ambos lugares está entre las más altas de los Estados Unidos. Nueva York y Massachusetts fueron para los estudiantes lo que Detroit en ese tiempo para los trabajadores de la industria automotriz.

Tampoco es sorprendente la época en que surgió, considerando la coyuntura en que se encontraba tanto la teoría como la historia.

Los tres autores estaban involucrados con una revista llamada *Zerowork*. La propuesta teórica de la revista era una síntesis entre la perspectiva "obrerista" (proveniente de Italia) y la campaña Sueldo para el Trabajo Doméstico iniciada en 1972 por el Colectivo Feminista Internacional. La perspectiva obrerista se arraigaba en las luchas de los obreros fabriles de un cordón industrial que se extiende desde Los Angeles, pasando por Detroit hasta Turín, mientras que las raíces de Sueldo para el Trabajo Doméstico estaban en las luchas de mujeres no remuneradas que exigían un sueldo por su trabajo doméstico en la casa, incluyendo la lucha por los "derechos de bienestar social" en los Estados Unidos.

Cuando se escribió *Sueldo para Estudiantes* ya había emergido una conciencia teórica de que "lo social" es un tipo particular de industria. En virtud de esas coyunturas teóricas el terreno estaba preparado también para sembrar un nuevo pensamiento sobre el trabajo de los estudiantes. Junto a esos influjos teóricos y políticos se debe considerar el impacto del cambio en el rol de las universidades según eran concebidas por el capital y su Estado.

Había sido un axioma de las políticas estatales de los años cincuenta y sesenta que las universidades servían para aumentar la productividad de la fuerza de trabajo y la disciplina social como vías de ascenso social, así como para auspiciar investigaciones para generar nuevas mercancías y métodos de producción. Así, hasta el final de los años sesenta tanto capitalistas como trabajadores consideraban que la educación era un "bien común". Pero ante las intensas luchas de los sesenta —por la libre expresión, por derechos civiles, por los derechos de la mujer, y contra el reclutamiento, contra la guerra de Vietnam y contra el uso de las universidades para investigación militar— se produjo un cambio decisivo en la actitud de la clase capitalista hacia la educación universitaria.

La huelga nacional de estudiantes contra la invasión de los Estados Unidos a Camboya, y los asesinatos de estudiantes por parte de soldados y policías en las universidades de Kent State y Jackson State en 1970, marcaron un punto de inflexión decisivo al respecto. El nuevo consenso capitalista fue que, en vez de producir una fuerza de trabajo confiable y calificada para las fábricas, oficinas y la milicia, las universidades de los Estados Unidos (recientemente "saneadas" de profesores de izquierda por las purgas macarthistas de los años cincuenta y principios de los sesenta) estaban engendrando masas de licenciados anti-imperialistas y anticapitalistas. De forma ilógica, estos rebeldes eran subsidiados por impuestos estatales y federales que en parte se recaudaban de las corporaciones. Eso tenía que parar. Ya en los años setenta las autoridades estatales y las corporaciones empezaron a demandar que los campus "conflictivos" no recibieran más financiamiento y que los estudiantes fueran forzados a pagar por *su propia* educación, la cual dejó de ser proclamada como un bien común.

No sabíamos en ese tiempo cómo nombrar tal cambio, pero estábamos conscientes de un desplazamiento hacia lo que pronto se llamaría la universidad "neoliberal", donde la educación se vuelve una mercancía que el o la estudiante compra, una inversión que hace en su futuro, y donde la institución misma sigue el modelo empresarial.

Esta neoliberalización de la universidad estaba apenas comenzando en 1975. *Sueldo para Estudiantes* describió y satirizó este desplazamiento.

Al momento de escribir el panfleto, los autores también participábamos del cambio que estaba ocurriendo al interior del propio movimiento estudiantil. Tras años de estar involucrados con "asuntos políticos", como el racismo en las políticas de admisión universitarias o el reclutamiento militar en los campus, hacia fines de los años setenta los estudiantes comenzaban a preocuparse de "asuntos economicistas".

Las protestas contra el desfinanciamiento de las universidades, contra el aumento de los aranceles y contra la disminución de la ayuda estudiantil (becas y subvenciones) se volvieron algo habitual en los campus. En retrospectiva, vemos que esta nueva movilización estudiantil intentaba detener la neoliberalización del sistema universitario estadounidense. *Sueldo para Estudiantes* brindó un idioma, un vocabulario a este nuevo movimiento estudiantil. En vez de describir a los estudiantes como consumidores o microempresarios que invierten en su futuro, los llamó *trabajadores*. Contra el aumento progresivo de los aranceles, exigió "sueldo para el trabajo estudiantil".

Sueldo para Estudiantes no fue sólo un "texto de reflexión" o un acto de provocación intelectual, aunque ciertamente cumplió ambas funciones. Junto a camaradas del círculo *Zerowork*, entre otros, los y las activistas de Sueldo para Estudiantes hicieron campaña en universidades por todo el noreste de los Estados Unidos.

La primera etapa de este trabajo político consistió en llamar la atención de los estudiantes sobre la perspectiva de Sueldo para Estudiantes. Presentamos la idea en conferencias de izquierda y en reuniones estudiantiles. Escribimos volantes, distribuimos autoadhesivos, participamos de manifestaciones en los campus y expusimos en los cursos de profesores simpatizantes. Rechazamos concebir programas concretos que definieran "cuánto" habría que pagar y "a quién" habría que entregar estos sueldos. La meta fue formar facciones de Sueldo para Estudiantes en las universidades y construir una red que, para empezar, cambiase el discurso de la izquierda (la cual en algunos sectores era hostil a la demanda) y también transformara lo que quedaba del movimiento estudiantil.

La campaña Sueldo para Estudiantes tomó como modelo la labor de la campaña en los Estados Unidos de Sueldo para el Trabajo Doméstico, que a mediados de los años setenta estaba alcanzando su cénit organizacional. Buena parte de su organización política fue dirigida contra los ataques a las mujeres que recibían beneficios sociales, ataques que en ese tiempo se hacían en nombre de "la crisis fiscal". La campaña denominó a los "beneficios sociales" como los primeros "sueldos para el trabajo doméstico".

Sueldo para Estudiantes aprendió de esta ampliación del concepto de sueldo y buscó aplicarlo al estudiantado. De la misma manera en que la campaña Sueldo para el Trabajo Doméstico consideró que los "beneficios sociales" eran una primera forma de remuneración para el trabajo doméstico, los y las activistas de Sueldo para Estudiantes notaron que las diversas ayudas financieras estudiantiles eran formas primarias de sueldos para estudiantes. Nos unimos a las manifestaciones y organizamos protestas contra los recortes a estas "ayudas", que entendíamos como "sueldo". En algunos lugares esta campaña logró integrar diversos sectores de la clase trabajadora, desde madres que recibían beneficios sociales y activistas de la comunidad, a estudiantes de posgrado, muchos de los cuales habían obtenido acceso a la universidad gracias a las luchas por los derechos civiles de la época. Aunque Sueldo para Estudiantes —como otras luchas por aumentos salariales— no era en sí misma una campaña revolucionaria, entendimos que el acto de ponerle fin al trabajo no remunerado en *todas* sus formas desestabilizaría, de hecho colapsaría, el sistema capitalista para el cual genera tanto plusvalor.

Como organizadores también entendimos que recibir un sueldo por nuestro trabajo estudiantil nos proveería del poder adicional necesario para, en turno, rechazar la mayoría del trabajo cotidiano que nos impone el capital, incluyendo aquel que se requiere para "costear" el hecho de ser puestos a trabajar en la escuela. Aquel trabajo nos negaba el tiempo para pensar, crear, compartir y cuidarnos unos a otros. Como aquellas personas que se organizaron para exigir sueldo para el trabajo doméstico, entendimos que el hecho de recibir un pago por las labores estudiantiles al final aumentaría el poder de los estudiantes para rechazar el trabajo impuesto por el capital.

Está claro, mirando atrás, que en los Estados Unidos el capital y su Estado entendió que la noción expandida e incluyente de sueldo, promovida por Sueldo para el Trabajo Doméstico y Sueldo para Estudiantes, era una amenaza política al sistema. No es casualidad que muchas de las reformas neoliberales de los últimos treinta años hayan sido ataques a los derechos de bienestar social y al acceso gratuito a la educación universitaria. Tampoco es casual que esos ataques hayan sido llevados a cabo tanto por demócratas como por republicanos a la par de recortes a sueldos y beneficios de los asalariados.

Como demanda, Sueldo para Estudiantes surgió durante la nefasta época en que los estrategas del capital norteamericano empezaron a abandonar la política keynesiana de subsumir las luchas salariales a los planes de desarrollo capitalista. Así, en vez de sueldo para los estudiantes tenemos un enorme aumento en los aranceles universitarios (500% desde 1985 al presente). El resultado es que, hoy, el estudiante deudor debe cerca de 30 mil dólares en promedio, mientras que el total de la deuda por préstamos estudiantiles asciende a más de 1.1 trillones de dólares. En vez de recibir sueldos por su trabajo, los y las estudiantes de los Estados Unidos siguen pagando por trabajar en las universidades y por ser capacitados para su futura explotación.

Por cierto es gratificante ver, cuarenta años después de su publicación, un interés renovado en lo que podría parecer una nota al pie hecha a contracorriente de la reforma neoliberal de la universidad. ¿De qué puede servir este panfleto para un movimiento estudiantil que de nuevo se levanta, ahora desde Chile hasta Quebec, incluyendo entre medio a muchas ciudades de los Estados Unidos? Cada movimiento debe decidir eso por sí mismo. Las respuestas de la nueva generación de estudiantes a las inquietudes de este panfleto proveerá un conocimiento político útil para todos nosotros.

Desde ya podemos notar, sin embargo, que *Sueldo para Estudiantes* puede cumplir por lo menos con un propósito: al mostrar que los y las estudiantes son trabajadores, y que lo que hacen en las universidades no es "consumir" un producto llamado "educación superior", el panfleto empodera la lucha contra la deuda estudiantil. Deja en claro que no son los estudiantes quienes le deben una cantidad gigantesca de dinero a las universidades, al gobierno y a los bancos. Son estas instituciones las que deberían estar pagándole a quienes estudian, dado que éstas —y, finalmente, el capital— prosperan sobre la base del trabajo estudiantil impago. En el período actual, cuando los políticos están proponiendo "soluciones" neoliberales a la crisis desatada por la deuda estudiantil —como por ejemplo los ranking de universidades para hacer de los estudiantes "mejores clientes en el mercado educacional"— *Sueldo para Estudiantes* responde que los y las estudiantes son trabajadores explotados y sin remuneración, obligados a realizar un trabajo que debe ser pagado.

Nueva York, 2015

Sueldo para Estudiantes

(Un panfleto en la forma de un cuaderno celeste, 1975)

Los Estudiantes de 'Sueldo para Estudiantes'

La fábrica de disciplina mental en 1965

"*Es de mañana. El señor del tiempo anuncia el alba e instala el sol (la lluvia, la nieve, las nubes, etcétera, lo que sea más apropiado) en el cielo. Y como un reloj mecánico la tierra hace tic-tac alrededor del sol una vez más*".

Fulano pertenece a la Unidad 12 de la Fábrica de Disciplina Mental de Elm City. Es Nuestro Ejemplo del día. Fulano es una persona Común y Corriente, o lo era hasta que Falló. Estaba sentado en Nuestra sala de necesidades físicas junto a otros productos en masa, sus colegas, con un lápiz en la mano derecha, un papel sobre la mesa, la mente puesta en su trabajo, ocupado.

A propósito, algunos antecedentes. El pretexto original para la existencia de Nuestra sala de necesidades físicas fue "producir y distribuir comida que supla Nuestras instrucciones disciplinarias con estímulo físico y semisatisfacción".

Pero su propósito ahora es servir como lugar de reunión para Fulanos, Sultanos y Menganos que no estén designados a nada más importante. Acá les enseñamos obediencia, una parte muy, pero muy importante de la disciplina mental total. Pero sigamos con Fulano. Estaba Bien hasta que descubrió la osadía de levantarse e ir directamente a Nuestra fuente de agua y tomar dos enormes tragos, llenando por completo su boca y aplacando su sed a expensas nuestras.

Ahora, todos Ustedes han sido disciplinados para darse cuenta de que ese no es el propósito de Nuestras fuentes de agua. Han recibido programación para que entiendan que están ahí como tentación disciplinaria y son parte de Nuestro Plan solo con ese propósito. Tienen que dominar su sed, no como Fulano. Él es malo, malo, malo. Uno de Nuestros supervisores tuvo que hacerlo escoltar hasta el médico cirujano, quien rápidamente le cosió los labios.

Algunos de Nosotros pensamos que el castigo a Fulano fue demasiado leve para una muestra de desobediencia tan deplorable. Pero Nosotros sí creemos en la compasión. Un Principio es un principio, pero de qué vale un principio si ignoramos lo humano.

Estudien la importancia de esto para la clase de mañana.

(Escrito en la escuela por un estudiante de secundaria)

¿Qué es el trabajo estudiantil?

Ir a la escuela, ser un estudiante, es un trabajo. Se le llama trabajo estudiantil, a pesar de que usualmente no sea considerado un trabajo real porque no recibimos sueldo alguno por hacerlo. Esto no significa que el trabajo estudiantil no sea trabajo, sino que nos han enseñado a creer que sólo si recibes un sueldo <u>realmente trabajas</u>.

El trabajo estudiantil se presenta en forma de múltiples tareas con intensidades variadas y diferentes combinaciones de labores calificadas y no calificadas. Por ejemplo: hemos de aprender a sentarnos silenciosamente en salas de clase por largos períodos de tiempo, sin perturbar a nadie. Hemos de escuchar con atención y tratar de memorizar lo que allí se dice. Hemos de obedecer a los profesores. De vez en cuando aprendemos ciertas habilidades técnicas que nos hacen producir más cuando trabajamos en empleos fuera de la escuela. La mayor parte del tiempo, sin embargo, lo pasamos realizando un montón de labores no calificadas.

La característica común de todas las tareas involucradas en el trabajo estudiantil es la Disciplina, esto es, trabajo forzado. A veces se nos disciplina, lo que quiere decir que otros (profesores, directores e inspectores) nos fuerzan a trabajar. Otras veces nosotros nos auto-disciplinamos, lo que quiere decir que nos forzamos a nosotros mismos a realizar el trabajo estudiantil. No es raro, entonces, que a las diferentes categorías del trabajo estudiantil solían llamárseles Disciplinas.

Obviamente es más barato y mejor para el Capital si nos disciplinamos a nosotros mismos, ya que esto ahorra dinero para pagar más profesores, directores, e inspectores que son trabajadores asalariados y deben recibir algún tipo de pago. Como estudiantes autodisciplinados, nosotros llevamos a cabo la doble tarea de hacer el trabajo estudiantil y de obligarnos a nosotros mismos a hacerlo. Es por esta razón que los administradores de las escuelas ponen tanto énfasis en los aspectos de auto-disciplinamiento, al mismo tiempo que intentan mantener los costos de disciplinarnos al mínimo.

Como todas las instituciones capitalistas, las escuelas son fábricas. Poner Notas y hacer Seguimientos son maneras de medir nuestra productividad dentro de la escuela-fábrica. No sólo se nos entrena para asumir nuestra futura "posición en la sociedad", sino que también estamos siendo programados para llegar al "lugar adecuado". La escuelafábrica es un escalón esencial en el proceso de selección que destinará a algunos a barrer las calles y a otros a supervisar a los que barren.

El trabajo estudiantil puede también incluir algún tipo de conocimiento que los mismos estudiantes encuentren útil. Este aspecto, sin embargo, está rígidamente subordinado al interés más inmediato del Capital: la disciplina de la clase trabajadora. Porque, al final, ¿qué beneficio tiene para el capital un ingeniero que habla chino y puede resolver ecuaciones diferenciales si siempre falta al trabajo?

¿Por qué el trabajo estudiantil?

La mayoría de los economistas están de acuerdo: "el trabajo estudiantil es un bien de consumo y un bien de inversión". Su respuesta a la pregunta de "¿por qué el trabajo estudiantil?" es que la educación que obtiene el estudiante involucra a este maravilloso bien de dos caras. No sólo se invierte en uno mismo de tal manera que en el futuro se obtenga un trabajo que pague bien, sino que además ¡es divertido! Esto está bastante lejos de aquellos días en que invertir significaba abstenerse, pero ¿podemos tomar esto en serio?

Consideremos el lado del "consumo". Dado que los economistas entienden por bien de consumo algo que se puede disfrutar, que es placentero y satisfactorio, entonces cualquiera que se refiera a la enseñanza como un bien de consumo debe estar hueviando.

La presión constante para terminar las tareas, el rollo de los horarios, las estúpidas noches en vela estudiando para exámenes, y el resto del auto-disciplinamiento que sucede en el intertanto, inmediatamente suprime cualquier posibilidad de diversión. ¡Es como decir que ir a la cárcel es un bien de consumo, porque es placentero salir de ahí!

Ciertamente uno podría decir que algo se disfruta yendo la escuela, pero no es realmente la educación. Más bien, es <u>la lucha contra esa educación</u> lo que se disfruta. Son los viajes que uno hace para capear las clases, las tomas y manifestiaciones que las suspenden, los encuentros amorosos que nos distraen, las conversaciones dispersas en bares, los libros incorrectos leídos, y los libros correctos leídos en los tiempos incorrectos: todo lo que uno hace para <u>no</u> educarse. Entonces, por el lado del consumo, la conclusión es exactamente la opuesta a la de los economistas.

¿Y qué pasa por el lado de la "inversión"? Durante la década de los sesenta, cundía entre los profesores de economía, los banqueros y los "orientadores" pedagógicos un acuerdo: la escuela era una buena inversión <u>personal</u>. La idea era que te administraras a ti mismo como a una pequeña empresa, como una mini General Motors, de tal forma que pudieras <u>invertir</u> en ti mismo yendo a la escuela, igual que una corporación compra maquinaria con el objeto de obtener mayor rendimiento, operando según el principio: tienes que gastar dinero (invertir) para hacer dinero. Si consigues levantar fondos (y achicar el estómago) para ir a la escuela, sea con un préstamo, trabajando en un segundo trabajo, o haciendo que tus padres paguen, puedes esperar sacar algún <u>provecho</u> de ese dinero, porque puedes obtener un trabajo mejor pagado en el futuro, considerando tu mayor escolaridad. En el auge de lo que denominaron "la revolución del capital humano", renombrados economistas plantearon que se consigue mayor rendimiento al invertir en la propia educación que comprando un lote de acciones de General Motors. ¡Esto era capitalismo para la clase trabajadora, con venganza y todo!

Fuera del disgusto que esta "visión inversionista" pueda provocar —según la cual, si eres una empresa, una parte de ti será un trabajador y la otra parte será el jefe de ese trabajador— uno podría preguntarse si efectivamente yendo a la escuela se obtendrá más dinero en el largo plazo. En los sesenta, todo el mundo aseguraba que así sería, pero en los setenta, ya "agobiados de crisis", se perdieron todas las apuestas. Las autoridades ahora están diciendo que sus análisis anteriores fueron malinterpretados, que no se puede esperar "rentabilidad" de una inversión hecha en uno mismo. Como era de esperar, resulta que no eres una operación de lucro más efectiva que General Motors. En el mejor de los casos, te saldrán con un <u>posible </u>incremento en lo que ellos llaman tu ingreso "psicológico", en tanto que si tienes mayor escolaridad, te puede tocar una pega más "amable", por no decir bien pagada; pero ni siquiera eso está garantizado, especialmente considerando que los trabajos "amables" y "decentes" están pasando a ser inciertos, difíciles de realizar e incluso, peligrosos, como por ejemplo, la docencia. Pareciera que los estudiantes son un error de planificación.

Es evidente para cualquier estudiante que la tentativa del "bien de inversión" por hacernos ver el beneficio de trabajar gratis o incluso pagar por trabajar en la escuela, es una gran farsa. Por eso se hace cada vez más difícil convencer a alguien de que desembolse dinero para la escolaridad, contándole el cuento de hadas de uno mismo como una lucrativa empresa. Y así, ambos lados de la afirmación de los economistas colapsan, pero en el medio de esta debacle, el trabajo estudiantil encuentra un nuevo defensor que emerge de un sector que podría parecer improbable: la Izquierda.

El profesor "socialista" y el estudiante "revolucionario" se han convertido en defensores acérrimos de la universidad pública frente a "recortes de presupuesto" y cosas similares. ¿Por qué? Su historia dice algo así: la educación conduce a la habilidad de hacer más y mejores conexiones respecto a tu situación en la sociedad, en una palabra, la educación te hace más "consciente". Dado que las universidades públicas abren la posibilidad de tener una clase trabajadora altamente educada, estas universidades permiten a la clase trabajadora tener mayor conciencia de clase. Además, una clase trabajadora más consciente prestará menos atención a demandas meramente "economicistas" de más dinero y menos trabajo, y podrá abocarse a la tarea política de "construir el socialismo". Esta lógica provee a la Izquierda tanto de una explicación a la crisis de la universidad —el Capital le teme a esa clase trabajadora altamente consciente que la universidad estaba empezando a engendrar— como también de una demanda: aumentar el trabajo estudiantil ¡y no lo contrario! Así, en nombre de la conciencia política y el socialismo, estos izquierdistas intensifican el trabajo estudiantil (que no es otra cosa que trabajo sin sueldo) y desaprueban las demandas de los estudiantes por reducirlo, denostándolas como un relapso capitalista. Mientras defiende el trabajo gratuito que se hace en las escuelas, la Izquierda aprovecha la ocasión para sacar a la clase trabajadora de su letargo "materialista" hacia su misión superior: la construcción de una sociedad socialista.

Pero la izquierda entra en conflicto al recordar la vieja pregunta planteada a anteriores eruditos iluminadores de la clase trabajadora: ¿quién educará a los educadores? Ya que la izquierda no parte de lo evidente, que la escuela es un trabajo no remunerado, todos sus esfuerzos llevan a más trabajo no remunerado para el capital, es decir, a más explotación. Todos sus intentos por aumentar la conciencia de clase parecieran no darse cuenta del control que ejerce el capital en su propio terreno, el de la misma Izquierda, y así acaba apoyando consistentemente los esfuerzos del capital por intensificar el trabajo, y por racionalizar y disciplinar a la clase trabajadora. De este modo la "construcción del socialismo" se convierte en una estrategia más para conseguir acrecentar el trabajo gratuito al servicio del capital.

Así, la defensa que hacen el capital y la Izquierda del carácter impago del trabajo estudiantil simplemente se va a la mierda.

Los estudiantes son trabajadores no remunerados

Los estudiantes pertenecemos a la clase trabajadora. Más concretamente, pertenecemos a esa parte de la clase trabajadora que no recibe sueldo (no remunerada). Nuestra falta de remuneración nos condena a una vida de pobreza, dependencia y exceso de trabajo, pero lo peor es que no recibir un sueldo significa que carecemos del poder que el sueldo proporciona cuando hay que tratar con el capital.

Sin sueldo estamos condenados a una vida de mera subsistencia. Se nos obliga a sobrevivir con lo que otros no tolerarían. La vivienda cuyo alquiler podemos pagar está hacinada y no cumple con mínimas condiciones de habitabilidad. La comida que comemos, que estamos obligados a comer, es la insípida comida institucional de las marcas más baratas. Nuestra ropa y entretenimiento son estandarizados y monótonos. Somos un evidente caso de pobreza.

Ya que no recibimos sueldo y dado que tenemos que vivir de algo, debemos sacar el dinero de otra parte, dependemos de alguien que sí recibe un salario. Para algunos estudiantes, la subsistencia y matrícula están al menos parcialmente cubiertas por algún familiar cercano. Como estudiantes sin sueldo, no obstante, estamos en una relación de dependencia con nuestros padres u otros benefactores, lo que nos deja <u>sin poder</u>. Además, si la familia entera se sacrifica —la madre obtiene un segundo empleo y el padre suda sangre para poder pagar la educación— nuestros padres son debilitados en su lucha contra el trabajo, mientras nosotros somos chantajeados para aceptar el trabajo estudiantil. A pesar de que trabajamos tanto como quienes reciben un sueldo, se nos obliga a depender de ellos; porque con la excepción de aquellos estudiantes que sí reciben un sueldo (en las Fuerzas Armadas, en la "ilustrada" Prisión de Lompoc en California, en los programas de entrenamiento de corporaciones privadas, en la Capacitación Manpower) la mayoría de los estudiantes no reciben sueldo alguno por el trabajo estudiantil que realizan.

Para aquellos de nosotros que no recibimos tal apoyo, carecer de sueldo significa obtener un trabajo adicional fuera de la escuela. Y como el mercado laboral está saturado de estudiantes en busca de estos trabajos, el capital nos impone salario y beneficios mínimos. Como resultado, trabajamos aún más horas, o incluso realizamos trabajos adicionales. Debido a que nuestro trabajo estudiantil no es pagado, la mayoría de nosotros trabajamos durante las así llamadas "vacaciones" de verano. Incluso si nos tomamos ese tiempo libre, no tenemos dinero para disfrutarlo. Este absurdo se magnifica a causa de las altas exigencias de productividad que constantemente se nos imponen como estudiantes (exámenes, pruebas, informes, etc.) y por el modo en que se nos programa para que nos autoimpongamos requisitos adicionales de productividad (trabajos extra para subir las notas, lecturas y reflexiones fuera de las programadas para nuestras clases —y no para nosotros mismos— capacitaciones laborales, ayudantías, etc.). Por un lado, somos forzados a trabajar por nada, y por el otro se nos obliga a hacerlo por casi nada.

Por supuesto, se nos dice que en el futuro todo será compensado. Dicen que conseguiremos un significativo y bien remunerado trabajo con secretaria incluida. Que nuestro trabajo gratis no será en vano. Pero, como sabemos, incluso antes de salir bailando alegremente de esta fábrica, sólo nos espera un deprimente trabajo de recepcionista en el Holiday Inn de la esquina o, en el mejor de los casos, terminar como secretarios en nuestro antiguo lugar de trabajo dentro de la universidad.

La realidad de la situación es que algunos estudiantes ya están empezando a ser remunerados por su trabajo estudiantil:

- En las Fuerzas Armadas; el ROTC (el cuerpo de entrenamiento para los oficiales de reserva de los Estados Unidos) paga la matrícula más $100 al mes por estudiar.
- Algunas corporaciones le pagan a sus empleados para ir a la universidad nocturna o por continuar sus estudios con posibilidades de obtener mayores grados académicos.
- Los carceleros de la Cárcel de Lompoc le están pagando a los reclusos por hacer trabajo estudiantil en la Universidad de California.
- Los clientes de los programas de Capaccitación Manpower reciben becas durante su capacitación.
- Los beneficiarios de Seguridad Social.
- Los becarios BEOG (Becas de oportunidades básicas de la educación).
- Los veteranos de Vietnam.

Sueldo para Estudiantes

Estamos hartos de trabajar gratis.

Exigimos dinero real ahora por nuestro trabajo estudiantil.

Debemos forzar al Capital, que lucra con nuestro trabajo, a pagar por nuestro trabajo estudiantil. Sólo entonces podremos dejar de depender de la ayuda financiera institucional, de nuestros padres, de nuestros segundo o tercer trabajo, y del trabajo de verano que hacemos para poder sobrevivir. Ya nos ganamos nuestro sueldo; ahora nos lo tienen que pagar. Sólo de esta manera lograremos alcanzar el poder que necesitamos para lidiar con el Capital.

Podemos hacer mucho con ese dinero. Primero, tendremos que trabajar menos ya que la "necesidad de trabajo" extra desaparecerá. Segundo, disfrutaremos inmediatamente de un aumento en nuestro estándar de vida, pues dispondremos de más recursos para gastar al tomarnos tiempo libre de nuestro trabajo estudiantil. Tercero, elevaremos el sueldo promedio de toda la zona afectada por nuestra presencia como trabajadores baratos.

Robándole este tiempo al trabajo estudiantil para exigir sueldos para estudiantes, pensamos y actuamos en contra del trabajo que realizamos. Además nos deja en una mejor posición para conseguir el dinero.

NO MÁS TRABAJO ESTUDIANTIL
NO REMUNERADO!

Los Estudiantes de 'Sueldo para Estudiantes'

Sueldo para los deudores, estudiantes para los prestamistas, vida para . . .*

16 Beaver, Nueva York
domingo 3 de marzo, 2013

René Gabri: Pensamos en un formato simple para esta noche. La idea es que Jakob Jakobsen diga algo de sí mismo y del trabajo que por un buen tiempo le ha interesado; al menos desde que lo conocemos, alrededor de diez años, un poco más. También qué lo llevó al panfleto *Sueldo para Estudiantes*, más algunas preguntas que tiene al respecto. Quizá entonces George Caffentzis y Silvia Federici nos pueden hablar un poco y atender a algunas de esas preguntas. Luego podemos, entre todos, reflexionar más allá, y plantear nuestras propias preguntas.

---

* Esta es la transcripción de un diálogo que se llevó a cabo en el espacio comunitario 16 Beaver durante el domingo 3 de marzo de 2013, a las 8 pm. La discusión duró dos horas y veinte minutos, y ha sido editada por motivos de extensión. Omitimos algunas divagaciones y comentarios repetitivos, pero la mayoría de lo ahí dicho está aquí transcrito, intacto.

Durante el evento se le hizo saber a los participantes que la discusión sería grabada. Dado que se trató de un encuentro público no fue posible identificar a todas las personas que intervinieron. De ahí la aparición en el texto de ocho "participantes no identificados".

Jakob Jakobsen: Gracias. En realidad hemos discutido bastante sobre la estructura de esta reunión, aunque con bastante relajo. Y todos estuvimos en desacuerdo, lo cual es un buen punto de partida para una discusión. Así que espero que esto sea más una tarde de conversa que una presentación. Y ojalá que la gente pregunte y hable cuando quiera . . .

RG: Y que interrumpa.

JJ: El motivo por el que, creo, estamos reunidos aquí esta noche es este folleto, *Sueldo para Estudiantes*, que encontré en la Feria Anarquista del Libro de Londres hace un par de años. Como conozco a Silvia y George, le escribí a Silvia para preguntarle si sabían algo de esto y Silvia respondió: "Sí, claro, es lo de George". Le pregunté a Silvia, porque *Sueldo para Estudiantes* se conectaba lógicamente con Sueldo para el Trabajo Doméstico, y dada la labor de Silvia ahí, imaginé que podría saber. Me interesé por el folleto —para hablar un poco de mí, pero no demasiado— porque llevo un buen rato investigando historias educacionales o luchas educacionales. Y he estado trabajando en la producción de un archivo para un proyecto de investigación sobre la Antiuniversidad de Londres, una universidad experimental nacida en 1968 que duró cerca de tres años; no está muy claro realmente cuándo se detuvo, lo que en sí revela algo respecto a su estructura experimental. Fue autoorganizada y dirigida por los mismos estudiantes. Esto también hizo que esta anti-institución lentamente se desinstitucionalizara y desapareciera del tejido social de Londres y del mundo. El motivo por el que creo importante hablar de estas cosas es para conectar ciertas luchas en el tiempo —el panfleto *Sueldo para Estudiantes* es de 1975—, y también conectar luchas en términos de espacio geográfico. He estado viviendo en Londres y siguiendo las luchas por la educación allá, y estaba muy interesado en venir aquí y hablar con George y Silvia, y con todos ustedes, y escuchar lo qué está pasando aquí en Nueva York. Así que esperaba más bien venir aquí a escuchar y no a hablar. Lo que sugeriría ahora, a menos que tengan otros planes, es que leamos este panfleto juntos.

Malav Kanuga: ¿Nos turnamos?

JJ: Sí.

[*Lectura colectiva del panfleto* Sueldo para Estudiantes]

JJ: Voy a volver a ti, George, pero quisiera empezar con una pregunta para ti, Silvia. Esta comprensión del estudio-trabajo como mano de obra en el marco de la economía capitalista, como mano de obra impaga, es —al menos para mí— una interesante idea a considerar. Y esto se vincula, por cierto, a la gran labor que has hecho y las luchas que has dado sobre la relación existente entre trabajo productivo y trabajo reproductivo. Donde "trabajo productivo" es trabajo reconocido y vinculado a un sueldo en la fábrica, mientras que "trabajo reproductivo" es el trabajo que de alguna manera sostiene la mano de obra productiva, como el trabajo doméstico, el trabajo estudiantil, etcétera. La pregunta interesante es sobre la relación entre el trabajo productivo y el trabajo reproductivo, ambos en términos de trabajo doméstico, pero también en términos de trabajo estudiantil. Entonces quisiera pedirte, Silvia, si puedes hablar sobre esta concepción de trabajo estudiantil como trabajo impago dentro de la producción capitalista.

Silvia Federici: Fue una consecuencia lógica de conceptualizar el trabajo doméstico como parte de un rango más amplio de actividades desde las cuales se produce la fuerza de trabajo. Fue al darme cuenta que hay una línea de ensamblaje que corre no sólo por las fábricas, sino que atraviesa la sociedad completa —los hogares, las escuelas— para producir trabajadores, quienes a su vez producen mercancías y ganancias. La redefinición de trabajo doméstico como un trabajo que produce fuerza laboral proporcionó una nueva perspectiva sobre la función de la escolarización. La escuela es una continuación del hogar; entrena y disciplina a los futuros trabajadores. Disciplinar a las nuevas generaciones es también un aspecto importante del trabajo doméstico. Esto es lo que lo vuelve tan difícil. No es sólo el trabajo físico, sino el hecho de que involucra una lucha constante, tener que decir "no", "no puedes hacer esto". La autodisciplina puede ser necesaria independientemente de la organización capitalista del trabajo, pero en la mayoría de los casos la disciplina que le enseñamos a nuestros niños es dictada por nuestras expectativas de lo que les pasará una vez que hayan entrado al mercado laboral. Es trabajo de las madres y los padres modelar nuestro deseo, asegurarse de que encajamos con las expectativas del mercado laboral.

Fue muy importante para las mujeres, y para el movimiento feminista, darse cuenta de esto, porque siempre hubo una tremenda culpa asociada a la idea de luchar contra el trabajo doméstico. El rechazo al trabajo doméstico conlleva mucha culpa porque las mujeres sentían que estaban socavando el bienestar de sus familias, el bienestar de las personas que se suponía ellas debían querer y cuidar. Así que ser capaz de identificar y desenredar aquellos aspectos del trabajo doméstico que son específicamente demandados para la producción de un trabajador, la producción de una persona cuyo destino es ser explotada, fue un proceso liberador. Empezamos a darnos cuenta de que podíamos reproducir gente para la lucha o que podíamos reproducirla para el mercado laboral. Obviamente la línea no es siempre tan clara, pero fue liberador porque hizo posible pensar que la lucha contra el trabajo doméstico no tiene por qué ser una lucha contra las personas que queremos.

Esa manera de pensar se trasladó a nuestra aproximación al trabajo estudiantil. En gran parte nuestro trabajo estudiantil, sea que estudiemos francés o matemáticas, es aprender a que nos disciplinen. Eso es lo primero que se espera que aprendamos. Sueldo para el Trabajo Doméstico permitió que viéramos cómo las escuelas nos preparan para trabajar en beneficio de nuestros futuros empleadores, y que vamos a la escuela sobre todo porque necesitamos un certificado, no por el placer de estudiar. Nos permitió ver que la manera en que una escuela se organiza está dictada por las necesidades del mercado laboral. También nos permitió entender las consecuencias de la dependencia económica de los estudiantes. Si tú no ganas un sueldo, entonces dependes de aquellos que financian tu manera de vivir, y en esa dependencia hay una relación de poder desigual. Algunas personas dicen: "Si tu marido gana un sueldo, entonces tú también tienes algo de dinero". Pero no es así. Cuanto sea el dinero que recibas, tienes que estar agradecido. No es algo que que te corresponde por derecho propio. Es lo mismo con los estudiantes. Cuando te ganas un sueldo por tu trabajo obtienes cierta autonomía, por lo menos con respecto a la familia y la comunidad. Pero si trabajas por nada, entonces tendrás que depender de otras personas. Además, cuando socialmente eres definido como trabajador no remunerado, como le pasa a estudiantes y trabajadores domésticos, entonces estás también destinado a convertirte en mano de obra barata y cada vez que obtienes empleo te pagarán menos que a otros trabajadores. Hay un estrecho vínculo entre la condición del trabajador doméstico y la condición del estudiante. Está claro que las personas del colectivo Zerowork que escribieron *Sueldo para Estudiantes* se inspiraron en Sueldo para el Trabajo Doméstico.

George Caffentzis: Sí.

SF: También es increíble ver cuán actual es todavía el panfleto. Particularmente en la primera parte se puede ver que ya estábamos confrontando una ideología neoliberal. Ya en los setenta había comenzado la idea neoliberal de la educación como una inversión en uno mismo, aunque no la podían implementar completamente hasta que desmantelaran el Estado de bienestar, la inversión del Estado en educación y en otras formas de reproducción.

JJ: Esto fue escrito . . .

SF: . . .en 1975, años antes de que floreciera completamente el neoliberalismo, pero en un contexto en que ya estaba escrito. Especialmente en Nueva York empezaban a decirnos: "No les debemos educación, ustedes deben pagar por ella".

JJ: Tal vez la gente acá sepa más, pero entiendo que fue en 1976 que CUNY (City University of New York) empezó a cobrar aranceles. En 1975, cuando se publicó esto, la universidad era gratuita. Pero George, lo que me llamó especialmente la atención en el texto fue la perspectiva de la "educación contra la educación". Actualmente en las universidades hay montones de luchas contra los recortes presupuestarios y contra la privatización, y para preservar la institucionalidad. Pero acá ustedes están criticando a la izquierda por aferrarse a un modelo institucional que es básicamente disciplinador, un modelo que está armando, formando y moldeando estudiantes para convertirlos en trabajadores obedientes. Acá aparece una corriente que podría considerarse más "anárquica", que no he visto mucho en el presente. La gente tiende a aferrarse a sus instituciones disciplinadoras, en vez de abandonarlas o desafiarlas radicalmente. No hay mucha autoorganización fuera y contraria a las instituciones, que use la "educación contra la educación" de la manera que ustedes propusieron entonces. ¿Tal vez podrías contarnos más sobre cómo surgió esto?

GC: El texto de *Sueldo para Estudiantes* fue escrito en 1975, al mismo tiempo que se estaba armando el primer número de *Zerowork*. Fue escrito por tres personas: John Willshire-Carrera, Leoncio Schaedel y yo. Ellos eran entonces estudiantes de posgrado en el Departamento de Economía de la Universidad de Massachusetts en Amherst. En ese tiempo yo todavía estaba trabajando en mi tesis de doctorado y enseñando en el Brooklyn College de la City University de Nueva York. Todos estábamos comprometidos con una política que articulaba lo que pensábamos eran dos revoluciones conceptuales y políticas. La primera era Sueldo para el Trabajo Doméstico, que destapó todo el universo del trabajo no remunerado. Esto tuvo un efecto profundo entre aquellos de nosotros que habíamos crecido en un contexto marxista que veía la mano de obra asalariada como el cimiento de la sociedad capitalista, y también a la clase trabajadora asalariada como la base de la transición hacia una sociedad más allá del capitalismo [*un ruidoso camión de la basura empieza a recolectar afuera. GC sube la voz mientras pasa*]. Esto creó toda una forma nueva de entender la naturaleza del trabajo. La segunda revolución conceptual y política situó [*casi inaudible*] el negarse a trabajar como el fundamento sobre el cual la lucha de clases opera.

Desde esta perspectiva la lucha de clases tiene en su raíz el rechazo al trabajo, no la identificación con el trabajo. Esto último había sido por largo tiempo uno de los pilares de una política marxista y de izquierda; por ejemplo, gran parte de la concepción liberadora de la educación se debe a esta identificación con el trabajo. El panfleto pone esta actitud en cuestión y sostiene que lo importante es cuánto *no* le entregamos al capital y cuánto rechazamos la identificación con ser el trabajador. Esto fue algo básico en nuestra manera de operar y pensar en *Sueldo para Estudiantes.* Déjenme tomar esta cosa. [*GC agarra el panfleto.*]

SF: La idea análoga era la izquierda diciéndole a las mujeres que encontrar un trabajo fuera de la casa era la manera de independizarse: "Encuentra un trabajo, súmate al sindicato, súmate a la lucha de clases. Así es cómo obtienes poder social y te vuelves parte de la clase trabajadora".

GC: Claro. Está de más decir, casi cuarenta años después, que tengo ya varias reflexiones sobre este panfleto. Tienen que considerar que la escritura, impresión y distribución del panfleto fue parte de una campaña política. Comenzamos como un pequeño grupo de personas y terminamos como un pequeño grupo de personas [*risas*]. Pero entre medio sí pasamos una cantidad de años revolviéndola por esa exigencia. Éramos parte de las luchas contra el cobro de aranceles en CUNY en 1976. Yo mismo estaba muy enojado con el Professional Staff Congress (Congreso de Empleados Profesionales), el sindicato académico de profesores de CUNY que negoció con la universidad en este asunto. Para mí era criticable el modo de acción del sindicato en ese momento, y de la izquierda en general, que veía las universidades como el vehículo por medio del cual ocurriría la liberación, como mencionaste, Silvia. Proponían la fábrica universitaria como un lugar de liberación, mientras nosotros argumentábamos que era tiempo de desvincularse de estas fábricas y empezar a decirles "no".

En el último tiempo he pensado especialmente en este panfleto por el trabajo que con mis camaradas hemos hecho con la campaña Occupy Student Debt y con Strike Debt. Desde el aventajado punto de vista del presente puedo ver cuán lejos hemos ido en esta lucha. Estábamos peleando por sueldos para los estudiantes en los setenta, y ahora estamos tratando de escapar de la esclavitud de la deuda; durante los últimos cuarenta años los estudiantes progresivamente se han echado encima una deuda enorme para ser explotados, literalmente. Este desenlace no pasó por accidente. Ya a finales de los sesenta y comienzos de los setenta los estrategas del capital, por ejemplo Gary Becker, estaban trabajando en un proyecto para una universidad neoliberal, antes de que el término "neoliberalismo" tomara su significado actual. Esto está documentado en *Sueldo para Estudiantes* y es una de las contribuciones del panfleto para el presente. Lo que ha pasado en los últimos cuarenta años es simplemente la aplicación de esa estrategia neoliberal hasta su lúgubre conclusión; y definitivamente reivindica la maldición de Thomas Carlyle a la economía como "una ciencia lúgubre". Conocemos el lúgubre final . . . Ahora que miro esta sala, estoy seguro de que la gente que veo está enfrentando un futuro lúgubre de repactaciones de deudas y morosidad ad infinitum. Este es el tipo de consecuencias que esperábamos poder detener e incluso revertir al momento de escribir el panfleto *Sueldo para Estudiantes*. Pero las fuerzas en acción eran demasiado poderosas.

SF: Así que ahora tienes que pagar para ser explotado. Tienes que pagar por el privilegio de ser entrenado para tu explotación futura. Es una doble explotación.

GC: Sí, es una locura.

JJ: Pero, continuando con la crítica a la institución educativa, básicamente concebida como una máquina disciplinadora, en lugar de adherir a la posición que reivindica la educación como un medio para que las personas de clase trabajadora asciendan en términos de clase, o como un medio de conscientización, ustedes no concibieron la educación como una vía a la liberación. Pienso que la crítica que ustedes hicieron al sistema educacional fue más absoluta, ustedes no estaban siendo pragmáticos sobre las posibiles ganancias que podría ofrecer la educación.

GC: A esas alturas nuestro argumento era que lo importante era la cuestión del poder y no la consciencia. Pensábamos que lo crucial era cambiar las relaciones de poder, las que para nosotros estaban arraigadas en la relación salarial. La discusión que desarrollamos en el panfleto, y que trasladamos a la campaña Sueldo para Estudiantes, era que la transformación verdadera de la universidad supondría una mayor capacidad de los estudiantes para organizar su propia conducta y básicamente romper con el trabajo de disciplinamiento, crucial para la educación capitalista. Ésa era la lógica, implícita y explícita en el texto, una lógica declarada abiertamente. Así que tienes razón, en ese sentido fue una crítica a la educación.

JJ: También si vinculamos esto a lo que está pasando hoy con la deuda, y con la esclavitud de la deuda, es posible ver el endeudamiento como medida disciplinadora.

GC: Claro, ¡doblemente!

SF: ¡Y las calificaciones! Debería escribirse un libro sobre la noche de calificaciones del profesor izquierdista. La noche "des-calificadora" del profesor de izquierda. He tenido tantas conversaciones con colegas de izquierda al respecto.

RG: ¿La noche descalificadora del izquierdista?

SF: Sí, la noche descalificadora del profesor izquierdista. Entiende alguien de qué estoy hablando?

Ayreen Anastas: Sí. Cuando tienes que entregar las calificaciones al día siguiente.

SF: Eso. Mañana tienes que calificar a tus estudiantes, pero eres un profesor consciente y sabes, claro, qué significa calificar. Sabes que es la esencia del sistema de clases. Sin embargo, tu idea de la educación es que puede ser *tan* inspiradora y con tanto potencial de alentar la revolución —podrías estar enseñando un curso sobre Marx— que quieres asegurarte de que los estudiantes se tomen en serio lo que enseñas. Entonces tienes que decidir si pondrás una B, o una B-, o una C+. Quizá incluso una C-, o una D. Hay personas que se pasan noches enteras tomando estas decisiones, queriendo ser justas con los estudiantes y con el curso, pero en general se abstraen del contexto en que se toman estas decisiones, que exige que hagamos una selección, y que la mayoría de las veces se basa en un criterio de clase. Este es uno de esos momentos en que la verdad sale a la superficie. El final del semestre en el curso sobre Marx y Revolución, [*risas*] cuando los estudiantes deben ser calificados. Aquellos que reprueban tendrán que tomar el curso otra vez y pagar más dinero; y si reprueban demasiados cursos tendrán que ir a barrer las calles. Hay muchas maneras en que podemos perder de vista lo que es la universidad, del sistema fábril, de la máquina de selección que es. La crítica acá no es tanto que muchos en la izquierda, de hecho todos nosotros en tanto aceptamos calificar, aceptamos este sistema, sino más bien que simulamos no estar contribuyendo a la selección, porque supuestamente los cursos que enseñamos llevarán a una mayor concientización. Es interesante por ejemplo que no haya habido una fuerte lucha en los Estados Unidos, por parte de los estudiantes o por parte de los profesores, para abolir el sistema de calificaciones. Algunos profesores radicales califican a todos con A, pero no es fácil hacerlo a menos que se dé una lucha. En Italia, en los setenta, los estudiantes fueron capaces de imponer la calificación grupal. No lograron abolir la calificación, pero impusieron la calificación grupal. Básicamente, quince a veinte personas daban un examen colectivo y recibían una sola calificación. Ahora eso ya no existe, pero durante algunos años se aplicó extensamente.

Participante no identificado 1: Hubo, en esa época, entre los estudiantes, otras instancias de trabajo colaborativo?

SF: Hubo un montón de trabajo colaborativo — por ejemplo, imponer un cierto currículum — decidir qué debía estudiarse. Y también estuvo la lucha por el *pre-salario*, análoga a sueldo para estudiantes.

JJ: La campaña Sueldo para Estudiantes se dirigió sobre todo a la dimensión económica de la vida estudiantil. A diferencia de los sesenta, en que se trataba más de liberación en general, en términos sexuales y de género, y muchas otras nuevas maneras de entender la liberación; en los setenta se volvió un asunto de dinero, de capital. Viendo la situación actual, por los suelos en términos de derechos de los estudiantes y de sus condiciones en la sociedad, me pregunto: ¿Mediante qué tipo de mistificación el capital ha sido capaz de salirse con la suya? Ha sido bastante significativa la operación de trasladar la discusión desde educación gratuita a mediados de los setenta a la esclavizante situación actual de la deuda estudiantil. Me pregunto qué tipo de mecanismos están operando en todo esto.

GC: Los mecanismos por los cuales esto sucedió tienen que ver, en cierto aspecto, con el final de la relación keynesiana entre clases que se desarrolla en los cincuenta y sesenta, y que entra en crisis en los setenta. Lo que empieza a pasar cada vez más es la transformación de la esfera de la reproducción en todas sus instancias, y no sólo para los estudiantes en las universidades. Así, por ejemplo, lo que pasó con los estudiantes en los setenta es similar a lo que pasó con el fin de los beneficios sociales.

SF: Eso es muy importante. El ataque al ingreso gratuito a la universidad, en los Estados Unidos, pasó al mismo tiempo que el ataque a las mujeres que recibían beneficios sociales. Todas las personas que recibían alguna asistencia desde el Estado, y sobre todo las mujeres que recibían Aid to Families With Dependent Children, AFDC (Ayuda a Familias con Hijos a Cargo), fueron vilipendiadas. Éste era un programa para madres que mantenían a sus hijos solas; ellas recibían alguna asistencia bajo la consideración de que criar es un trabajo, y que "la sociedad" se beneficia con la inversión en las nuevas generaciones. Pero en los setenta se montó una campaña masiva que denigraba a las mujeres que recibían beneficios sociales como "aprovechadoras", "parásitas", "farsantes". Había un fuerte elemento racial en eso, porque la mayoría de las mujeres que lucharon por los beneficios sociales eran negras, aunque la mayoría de las que los recibían eran blancas. Fue el comienzo de un camino largo que, en 1996, llevó a la abolición del sistema de bienestar social bajo Clinton, y cada vez más a la denigración de las personas acogidas al sistema de Previsión Pública. Hoy participar de la Previsión Pública es visto como algo socialmente destructivo. Las personas mayores son prácticamente acusadas de llevar el país a la bancarrota y de destruir el futuro de las nuevas generaciones, a pesar de que el dinero de la Previsión Pública ha sido deducido de sus sueldos.

GC: Esto se llevó a cabo en muchas, muchas etapas. Efectivamente los primeros pasos a nivel universitario empiezan con una manera nueva de organizar, por ejemplo, el modo de financiamiento de las universidades, lo que transformó completamente la manera en que las universidades operan. Lentamente empezaron a volverse máquinas alimentadas por aranceles pagados, hasta convertirse muy abiertamente en expresión de estructuras empresariales. Esto a pesar de presentarse a sí mismas como organizaciones sin fines de lucro, instituciones públicas; cosa que hacen incluso las universidades privadas. En ese sentido empiezan a crear un ambiente que opera con una lógica propia. Una vez que creas una situación donde la universidad sólo puede operar cobrando aranceles a sus estudiantes, entonces su lógica interna llevará al aumento perpetuo de esos aranceles. Esto tiene una matemática. No hay "vía de escape". Así que empezamos a tener este tipo de sistema universitario, que nos trae a la situación actual, y que empeora con la crisis financiera y económica. Y para sobrevivir a la crisis los aranceles universitarios siguen aumentando y crean millones de microcrisis para los estudiantes y sus familias.

JJ: George, has mencionado también, en otra parte, que en los sesenta hubo mucho dinero estatal invertido en las universidades, y a cambio lo que recibió fue rebelión, así que en los setenta el Estado se retiró del campus. Entendieron que el capital era aun mejor disciplinador que el Estado. El dinero es la mejor manera de disciplinar a las personas. Podría decirse que esa fue la conclusión de los sesenta.

GC: Y funcionó en un sentido muy importante. La transformación de las universidades es algo muy claro para todos, ahora es algo sabido. Nuestra crítica a la vida estudiantil es ya parte del sentido común. Ya no se trata de esa crítica, sino de qué vamos a hacer al respecto, porque la situación se ha vuelto muy radicalmente contra el poder de los estudiantes para determinar sus propias vidas.

RG: Hay otra dimensión de estas dos luchas —sueldos para el trabajo doméstico y sueldos para el trabajo estudiantil— que es muy interesante. La exigencia por sueldos para un tipo particular de fuerza laboral, que no es vista como fuerza laboral, es un horizonte para un tipo de lucha que puede transformar el escenario en sí. Porque aunque digas, George, que ahora es de conocimiento común, no sabría decir qué partes de estas luchas han ingresado al conocimiento común. Estoy seguro de que muchos de nosotros no sabíamos de esta lucha por sueldos para el trabajo estudiantil, y me pregunto qué aspectos de estas campañas todavía tienen potencia. Las luchas actuales tienden a reaccionar en contra, por ejemplo, del aumento de los aranceles. Pero, ¿cuál sería el horizonte de la lucha hoy? ¿Qué tipo de lucha podría transformar el escenario actual, o nuestra manera de ver la situación hoy? Parte del problema pareciera ser el modo en que percibimos la situación.

Alan Smart: Algo que llama la atención en el panfleto es que durante la crisis de los setenta

ya no era posible encontrar "buenos empleos".
Pareciera hacer referencia al conjunto de profundas implicancias de la situación posindus-
trial de Occidente. Ahora vemos cómo éstas
han avanzado mucho más. Ahora, al menos en
la retórica, no sólo los beneficios sociales son
percibidos como limosnas parasitarias, sino
cualquier exigencia de pago. El trabajador que
confía en ser pagado por hora es percibido
como alguien que no es lo suficientemente
entusiasta. Tu mención de esta nueva retórica
"emprendedora", donde cada persona no sólo
es una pequeña empresa, sino también un
"startup", un "artista", un "trabajador creativo".
Este tipo de trabajo es en realidad, bajo el viejo
modelo industrial, pura reproducción; la administración es reproductiva, los financieros son
reproductivos. Entonces lo que que se suprime,
se reniega, se oculta en paraísos fiscales, o se en-
vía a China, es la *producción* real de las cosas. Si
el trabajo reproductivo de baja gama es la labor
doméstica que nos permite seguir trabajando,
el lado alta gama de todo esto son las finanzas,
la administración, y el marketing, que permiten
tener éxito a la empresa. Pareciera que esa bre-
cha se ha reducido, de manera que todos somos
ahora emprendedores y freelancers trabajando
frente a nuestros laptops, en nuestra ropa interior, en los dormitorios que arrendamos y

vamos limpiando mientras trabajamos. Y se considera de mala educacion hablar cosas como el sueldo que obtienes por tu trabajo o de lo que sea que estás produciendo. En el auge de los noventa la idea era que, si eras exuberante y joven, te financiarían desde Wall Street, atravesarías todos los obstáculos, tendrías éxito, lo que era un especie de don. No era ya una deuda, sino algo así como una participación accionaria, un "riesgo". Ahora la explotación . . .

SF: Ahora la explotación está oculta.

AS: Siento una especie de nostalgia por la potencial negatividad de un sueldo, cuando un trabajador asalariado no está en riesgo. E incluso si la gente para la que trabajas gana mucho más dinero por tu fuerza laboral que tú, sabes que si pierden una apuesta, o si la embarran, de todas maneras te tienen que pagar. En cambio ahora todo es emprendimiento, y se espera que hagas tus "propuestas de negocios" en tu tiempo libre.

SF: Y tienes que enfrentar a tus empleadores solo.

JJ: Estaba leyendo sobre una compañía donde el 60% de los trabajadores eran estudiantes en práctica, sin sueldo. Ahí se me ocurrió que tal vez en diez años los practicantes tendrán que pagar para ir a trabajar [risas]. Ésta es la lógica de lo que pasó en la universidad. Nos dicen que es un privilegio ir a trabajar. Así que pronto existirá una estructura de pagos, donde podrás tener un trabajo increíble si pagas lo suficiente.

SF: Las universidades son las que están constantemente alimentando de estudiantes en práctica a esas compañías. Más y más cursos hoy requieren una práctica laboral. De esta manera la universidad puede extraer mano de obra no sólo directamente de los estudiantes, sino indirectamente a través del sistema de prácticas laborales. Es sabido que algunas compañías han despedido a sus trabajadores debido a que consiguen estudiantes en práctica desde las universidades.

RG: Sería bueno si los estudiantes que hay aquí de cualquiera de las universidades —sé que hay porque conozco a algunos—, si pudiesen intentar relacionar algunas de las preguntas planteadas en este panfleto con sus condiciones y luchas contemporáneas.

Persona no identificada 2: Algunos de nosotros vamos a Cooper Union. En realidad yo acabo de terminar, y lo que pasó en 1976 en CUNY nos está pasando a nosotros ahora mismo. Así que la pregunta sobre qué transformaría el escenario, o qué clase de poderes tenemos para oponernos a la colegiatura, cómo resistirla... La comunidad completa de ex estudiantes y egresados se opone a la estructura de aranceles, pero los que están en los altos cargos de los consejos directivos son gente de negocios, no nos considera como interlocutores, y siguen un modelo capitalista que llaman "realista". Ésta es una situación inminente para nosotros. Entonces, si ustedes tienen una *respuesta* a esa pregunta... [*Risas*].

Leo Caione: Quiero colgarme de lo que dijo Rene. Yo, justamente, fui estudiante en Venecia, soy italiano, y lo que quiero plantear respecto al panfleto es que existe un cambio en términos de tiempo. Puedo darles una especie de testimonio. No quiero hablar de mí, nada más usaré mi experiencia como ejemplo. Soy anacrónico porque vengo de una generación que tuvo que trabajar para ir a la escuela. Esto cuando era muy chico, a los once años. Ahora los estudiantes están muy malcriados. Veo estudiantes universitarios que no valoran las cosas que yo valoré: la posibilidad de estudiar. El panfleto tiene casi cuarenta años y el punto de vista ha cambiado mucho. En ese tiempo quizás muchas de las cosas planteadas eran ciertas, pero hoy los estudiantes están malcriados. ¡No quieren hacer nada!

Persona no identificada 3: Seguramente hay gente malcriada en todas las generaciones. No me parece que puedas hacer esa generalización.

LC: Quiero decir, hay profesionales hoy que —para obtener su educación— tuvieron que hacer sacrificios de los cuales no tenemos idea.

Persona no identificada 4: También hay un cambio, para esquivar este punto más moralista, en tanto el espacio de la educación se ha vuelto transaccional. Un espacio donde los estudiantes se han vuelto "clientes engreídos" porque están pagando por una clase. Algo sí ha ocurrido en el espacio educacional en relación a eso.

SF: Lo siento, pero llevo cuarenta años en el sistema educacional en este país y lo que dices no es mi experiencia. Los estudiantes a quienes he enseñado trabajaron mucho y sí se sacrificaron. No eran "malcriados". Cuando alguien tiene tres trabajos, además de estudiar, para pagar aranceles y otros costos, está sacrificándose.

Persona no identificada 5: Me parece intrigante cómo es que los estudiantes, tengan una educación gratuita o estén pagando 50 mil dólares al año en el New School, de alguna manera siempre algún segmento de la sociedad los retrata como "malcriados". Que esto suceda aunque tengas tres trabajos, seas deudor de miles de dólares, o estés "disfrutando" de educación gratuita es en sí un fenómeno fascinante. Solíamos tener algo así como un principio según el cual existía un *derecho* a la educación, y según el cual la sociedad le debe a su generación más joven algo como eso. Es posible tener la experiencia de estudiantes "malcriados", pero éste es un discurso que en realidad opera sólo para obstaculizar un análisis compartido de la explotación, transversal a grupos como los estudiantes o la clase trabajadora.

Nunca había escuchado la propuesta de Sueldo para Estudiantes. Soy del Reino Unido, donde todavía hay tomas universitarias en curso, aquí y allá. Incluso ahora, aunque la ola de manifestaciones estudiantiles fue hace dos años, la lucha continúa. Creo que es exactamente lo que hay que hacer a estas alturas, cuando las personas están cada vez más en esta línea populista de ataque donde esta situación de disciplina y deuda se retrata, de algún modo, como un privilegio. Precisamente cuando las personas dicen "bueno, si quieres tomar ese camino, ahora tendrás que pagar 9 mil libras al año en aranceles..." Eso es decadencia. Incluso los periodistas de derecha están diciendo que ya no es una inversión tener un título universitario.

Es fantástico como respuesta, en el momento preciso en que nos empiezan a cobrar tres veces más en aranceles, decir "en vez de eso, exigimos sueldos por este trabajo". Me parece una propuesta política realmente apasionante. Estoy contenta de haberla escuchado, leída de esta manera. Debe haber sido algo maravilloso oír su panfleto leído así [*risas*].

GC: Le aseguro que cuando lo escribimos en esos años, arriba de la mesa de cocina, no teníamos idea que sería un asunto de interés décadas después. En todo caso, hay partes de esta historia de lo sucedido entre 1975 y 2013 sobre las cuales es necesario reflexionar. No estoy seguro si ha sido contado ya, o siquiera si se ha pensado concienzudamente al respecto. Pero vale la pena hacerlo.

Participante no identificado 6: Siento que falta algo en la discusión. La pregunta "¿Qué hacemos?" ¿Podríamos re-examinar el valor de la educación desde el punto de vista del trabajador más que del capitalista? Pienso que es importante entender la diferencia entre el proceso del trabajo y el proceso del aprendizaje, e intentar hacer una distinción entre ambas cosas. También, en relación a esta idea de los estudiantes malcriados, o la manera en que la naturaleza misma de la educación ha cambiado en los últimos cuarenta años, y el modo en que la educación como mercancía es consumida de diferente manera que entonces. La producción misma de esa mercancía dicta el modo en que la consume el estudiante. Me parece que exigir sueldos no es necesariamente algo bueno. Te siguen explotando aun cuando estás recibiendo sueldo.

RG: En parte esas preguntas son abordadas en un texto que Silvia escribió en 1974, "Sueldo contra el Trabajo Doméstico," donde habla más claramente sobre cómo el sueldo no es el objeto de la lucha. Hablar sobre sueldos es también abrir el campo de acción y entender esas relaciones de manera muy diferente. Hay ahí una pregunta sobre aprendizaje versus trabajo. En cierto sentido, por la actual intermitencia del empleo, parte de la manera en que el capitalismo funciona, tienes que estar reformulando constantemente lo que sabes y cómo lo sabes entre los horarios en que eres remunerado, entonces ese aprendizaje está imbricado al proceso del mercado y se adapta a eso. Quizá alguien aquí está preparándose para presentar algún nuevo curso y está recogiendo ideas. Nunca sabes qué será lo que te consiga el siguiente empleo o "pega" o lo que sea. Se hace cada vez más difícil separar el lugar de aprendizaje del lugar de trabajo. Esto en la medida que trabajar en estas partes sobredesarrolladas del mundo requiere más y más de un cierto tipo de conocimiento, que además cambia continuamente para adaptarse a las circunstancias a su vez cambiantes.

JJ: Pienso que a lo que apuntaba George es que conocimiento es, en realidad, disciplina, y todo el asunto de los "estudiantes malcriados" se vincula al hecho de que los estudiantes tienen harto poder al interior de las universidades porque ahora son consumidores. Los cursos no se realizan si no hay diez estudiantes que se inscriban. La jerarquía de poder dentro de la universidad ha cambiado, desde un punto de vista neoliberal está centrada en el estudiante. Pero también es posible plantear que esto funciona como una herramienta disciplinaria, ahí los estudiantes son básicamente formados como consumidores, y se comportan como consumidores porque están pagando por sus estudios. Aprender en este contexto es más un disciplinamiento neoliberal, hasta donde puedo ver, los estudiantes aquí presentes me pueden corregir. Este cambio en la concepción del estudiante, ahora definido en términos de "pago tanto, y puedo exigir tales cosas", también está estructurando hoy la universidad.

Alexander Dwinell: También en relación a esta idea de la "auto-inversión", pareciera que el único motivo para la educación es capacitarte para trabajar. Pero no siento que muchas de las habilidades que aprendes en la universidad tengan relación directa con lo que haces en determinado empleo, sin embargo no puedes obtener ese empleo sin hacer el sacrificio físico de endeudarte. Cada vez más esta preparación para el trabajo pareciera ser el único motivo por el que se alude al valor de la educación. Eso obstaculiza nuestra capacidad para hablar sobre el valor real de la educación. Incluso en Cooper Union el discurso parece ser "tenemos que cobrar matrícula porque el mercado financiero ha cambiado y ahora no podemos proveerla sin cobrar", sin meterse nunca en las razones por las cuales alguna vez hubo acceso gratuito a la educación.

Participante no identificado 7: Es gracioso el modo en que circula la palabra "malcriado". En la lucha en Quebec *ese* fue el ataque principal de parte del periodismo convencional al movimiento estudiantil: que eran "niños malcriados". Es interesante porque, ¿qué es un niño malcriado? Un niño malcriado es un niño indisciplinado, uno que no hace lo que le dicen, ¿cierto? De ahí viene, y luego se mete la palabra en la discusión sobre estudiantes universitarios. Me ha tocado enseñar a montones de estudiantes que se sientan al fondo y empiezan: "ay no, ya está hablando de Marx de *nuevo*". Uno podría tildarlos de "malcriados" pero comencé a reflexionar al respecto, y a conversar con ellos y ellos están comprando una educación. Están comprándose una credencial. La mayoría de los estudiantes con que he hablado tienen la sensación de que los elementos más críticos del currículo son un impedimento a su habilidad para su futuro desempeño y no una ayuda. ¿Entonces qué pasa si "la flojera" o "la indisciplina" es en verdad una forma de resistencia incipiente que aún no ha sido organizada? Que pasa si lo que nos están diciendo es: "A la sociedad en la cual voy a graduarme le importo un carajo, entonces ¿para qué molestarme? ¿Qué le debo a esa gente? ¿Por qué debo esforzarme?" Es muy tentador pensar que deberíamos estar organizándonos con los estudiantes mateos, entusiasmados con la escuela y por aprender. Sin embargo pienso que deberíamos trabajar con la gran mayoría de los estudiantes, ahora en el sistema, quienes no son malcriados, sino increíblemente disciplinados y explotados. El problema no es que los estudiantes no sean lo suficientemente disciplinados, sino que aún no están lo suficientemente enojados.

RG: Me parece que perdemos de vista un aspecto del panorama que, como dice Leo, es la dimensión de clase. Es fácil descartar la idea del "estudiante malcriado", pero incluso según mi perspectiva, viniendo de un contexto de inmigrantes pobres mi primera experiencia universitaria fue exactamente "estoy rodeado de niños malcriados". Sentí un tremendo peso pensando "hay gente soportando vidas realmente de mierda para que yo pueda estar en esta escuela y supuestamente obtener una vida mejor". Esas condiciones de vida de verdad forman la manera en que percibes a la gente que te rodea, y me permite entender cómo puedes estar en esa posición y ver a los demás como antagonistas o como gente ajena a ciertos principios de realidad. Podemos dar la vuelta a esto, y decir que quienes estudian trabajan increíblemente duro, o que eso que percibimos como malcrianza es una especie de resistencia. Ambas cosas son verdad y no estoy en desacuerdo; sin embargo sigue existiendo una división de clases, en el sentido de que aquellos que vienen de entornos más acaudalados y aquellos que vienen de entornos más de clase trabajadora, o son inmigrantes, perciben lo que es estar en la universidad de maneras muy diferentes. No es algo dado. Así que es fácil para aquellos que ven cómo gente acaudalada participa de una toma, decir despectivamente "pueden hacerlo porque tienen padres ricos, pero en definitiva yo tengo que encontrar trabajo, y tengo un cerro de mierda que resolver, cuentas y deudas". También estamos luchando contra esto. No podemos eludir esas divisiones en la discusión, sino que tenemos que encontrar una manera de abordarlas. Y puede ser complicado cuando has vivido experiencias de empobrecimiento severo y llegas aquí y piensas "está muy bien aquí, hay muchísimas oportunidades en comparación con el lugar de donde vengo". Discrepo con la opinión de que todos los estudiantes son unos malcriados, pero tenemos que tomar consciencia de que la clase social es un problema importante.

LC: No quiero que se malentienda lo que dije sobre los estudiantes malcriados. Sé que hay gente, como yo, que ha mantenido tres trabajos para estar en la universidad.

AA: Pero el debate es sobre la situación más amplia. Dijiste "no quiero ponerme en el centro". Es importante salir de tu experiencia, es importante ir más allá de tu experiencia. También pensar *con* los otros: ¿quiénes son los otros con quienes puedo pensar? ¿Cómo puedo cambiar esta situación?

GC: En los cuarenta años entre la primera publicación de este panfleto y hoy, he visto con mis propios ojos y he sentido en mi piel la derrota de las políticas expuestas en este panfleto, y las consecuencias de esa derrota. Me tomó bastante tiempo entender las profundas consecuencias para mis estudiantes. A fines de los noventa y en los primeros años de este siglo lo que empezó a pasar es que mis estudiantes, que asisten a una universidad proletaria en Maine, no sólo tienen que pagar cada vez más aranceles que empezaron a subir más rápido que la inflación, sino que también están empezando a enfrentar un endeudamiento eterno, nuevo para ellos y sus familias. Obvié por varios años esta transformación. No vi lo que le estaba pasando a mis propios estudiantes. Yo era como ese "buen" profesor radical que se pasaba muchas noches calificando si un estudiante entendió el concepto de la alienación del trabajo en Marx, ¡sin reconocer realmente que esos estudiantes tenían que hacerse cargo de una deuda enorme para poder estar en mi clase y estudiar la alienación! En los últimos años he empezado mi penitencia, he empezado a comprometerme para cambiar esto. Lo que pueda hacer, lo he tratado de hacer —con algunos camaradas que veo acá— en la campaña Occupy Student Debt y en otros esfuerzos como Strike Debt, para denunciar esto.

Estoy hablando de un problema generalizado entre una gran mayoría de estudiantes: para ir a la universidad tendrán que endeudarse cada vez más. Éstas son consecuencias, según puedo ver, que tienen un efecto tremendamente desalentador. Si las luchas actuales contra la deuda estudiantil y en pro del libre acceso a la educación universitaria no tienen éxito, toda una generación quedará imposibilitada de organizar luchas autónomas contra el capital. Uno de los primeros pasos para cambiar este resultado es cambiar el vínculo entre los deudores de préstamos estudiantiles y las fuerzas que los tienen entre sus garras. En esta discusión parece vital que, antes de comenzar a pedir sueldo para los estudiantes, nos deshagamos de la deuda que los estudiantes están enfrentando en este momento.

JJ: Parte del ethos de su panfleto es contra la educación. De alguna manera me desconcierta el hecho de que sabiendo todo esto tantos estudiantes —todos nosotros, en algún sentido— igualmente participamos de la universidad, esta fábrica de disciplinamiento, conscientes de lo que va a pasar.

GC: El punto era que queríamos transformar esa alienación en un poder. Es decir, en lugar de la alienación como condición de derrota, lo que intentábamos hacer, mediante la transformación del proceso de estar en la universidad en una relación salarial, era por un lado reconocer el trabajo estudiantil como explotación, y por otro, que el o la estudiante reconozca su propia alienación en ese trabajo. En tal sentido sí, *Sueldo para Estudiantes* está en contra de la educación. Pero hay otra ironía en esto, porque es exactamente en ese proceso de alienación donde aprendes qué es la lucha y donde puedes empezar a luchar. Hay un giro sobre un giro en esto.

JJ: La lucha *es* una escuela. La educación es lucha, no obediencia.

GC: Exactamente... Suceden cosas parecidas en el trabajo reproductivo de la casa.

JJ: A los amigos de Cooper Union, sólo para saber: ¿están discutiendo si dejar la universidad o si mandar a la mierda la universidad? ¿Tal vez organizarse entre los estudiantes y hacer su propia universidad?

Participante no identificado 8: Por ahí va lo que pienso, pero realmente no hemos imaginado futuros posibles.

Victoria Sobel: Provengo de un entorno parecido al de Rene y asisto a una universidad gratuita. La mitad de mi familia es primera generación de inmigrantes, la otra mitad son inmigrantes de segunda generación. Pienso que un análisis de clase de lo que está sucediendo es crucial. Hay dos asuntos en juego. Está la estratificación de aquellos que pueden permitirse pagar por ir a la univerdad, sentarse y estar ahí. Y están aquellos cada vez más endeudados por ir a la universidad. Sobre la lucha estudiantil, concuerdo con que entrar al espacio académico o no depende de la clase y del accesso que uno tenga. Es interesante lo que decías sobre los estudiantes privilegiados tomándose sus escuelas. En mi caso, y en el caso de muchos de mis pares, en realidad era lo contrario; tal vez yo era uno de los estudiantes más marginales y endeudados. No estoy en posición de permitirme que esto continúe. Como se puede ver, ambas partes, los estudiantes más endeudados y aquellos que sí tienen esa posición, y que siempre han tenido esa posición, se alzan. Se trata o de unir ambas partes y reclamar esa posición y tomarse esos espacios, que es lo que pienso estamos tratando de hacer en nuestra universidad, o quizás, empezar algo nuevo.

Graeme Thomson: Si la educación se está volviendo una mercancía cuyas ganancias

disminuyen progresivamente versus endeudamiento, en un marco institucional, está cantada
la pregunta: ¿no debería la educación salirse
de la institución? Al menos en los términos en
que valoramos la educación. Pareciera que uno
se está lanzando de manera casi suicida a esta
situación de endeudamiento. Sobre todo mientras más nos preguntamos: ¿cuál es el valor de
tener un título? No te lleva a ninguna parte, y
el horizonte emancipatorio ya no está. Así, ¿por
qué la gente todavía considera que educación
y universidad son equivalentes, si el valor está
cada vez más lejos de ahí?

SF: En muchos casos es desesperación, porque
no puedes conseguir trabajo a menos que tengas cierto certificado. Aunque tengas pocas posibilidades de conseguir trabajo con eso, sabes
qué es lo que debes hacer. No tienes demasiadas
opciones. Es por esto que las personas siguen
queriendo ese certificado y pagan para eso, con
la esperanza de que les dará alguna seguridad.

AD: También está el factor de las universidades privadas en esta lucha. Me parece que no
hemos hablado lo suficiente sobre ellas en esta
discusión. Es ahí donde se está acumulando
una parte significativa de la deuda estudiantil,
para conseguir títulos de menor valor aún en

muchos casos. Es realmente como los embargos hipotecarios, algo como: "bueno. Te daremos crédito por un período acotado de tiempo, para que quedes absorbido completamente por este sistema, y luego te lo vamos a robar todo, aunque de todas maneras tendrás que pagarnos". Están atrapando completamente a la gente, aniquilando la posibilidad de pensar en cualquier otra cosa que no sea sobrevivir el día a día.

Themis Pellas: Ignoro si alguien acá estuvo en el sindicato estudiantil que se reunió el semestre pasado, pero ahí discutimos cómo ir más allá de un sindicato estudiantil hacia un sindicato más amplio de trabajadores de la ciudad. Esto significa entender que tanto estudiantes como trabajadores van y vienen por este mismo puente, y no olvidar que lo que las universidades están haciendo es prepararnos para las profesiones que vendrán. Así que es necesario trabajar en ambas orillas, y también entre medio. Cómo intervenir en esta compleja situación? Interviniendo en todas estas posiciones, diría yo. Esto significa que tienes que crear las profesiones que quieras mientras estás en la universidad. Algo interesante está pasando en Occupy, porque gente de diferentes universidades está tratando de entender nociones de reciprocidad con otras personas: "¿de qué manera les puedo ser útil?"

Si quiero ir más allá de las instituciones, tengo que reorganizarme. Tenemos que realizar estas luchas más amplias.

SF: Ayuda hacer el paralelo entre educación y el sistema de salud, porque puedes hacer el mismo razonamiento. Puedes decir: "Hay un montón de personas ricas que no lo necesitan, así que no deberíamos tener un sistema de salud público para todos". De hecho se dice eso todo el tiempo. Pero también podemos decir: "Debemos crear un sistema de salud fuera del mercado. Las personas están tratando de crear alternativas, porque sabemos que el sistema de salud que tenemos no está bien. Igualmente no podemos abandonar el sistema médico que hay porque aún no tenemos los medios para reemplazarlo. Veo la lucha por la educación y por el sistema de salud como parte del mismo proceso. Hay diferentes caminos para empezar a cambiarlos. Si los vemos como algo inamovible, estamos perdidos. Los estudiantes no están solos, tenemos que ver su lucha en un contexto más amplio. De otra manera no podemos ir más allá de las tácticas específicas, y eso es una derrota.

JJ: Sólo una cosa más sobre educación autoorganizada. En Dinamarca tuvimos la Universidad Libre de Copenhagen y el Estado dictó una ley para proscribirnos: nos prohibió usar el término "universidad". Al capital le asusta que los estudiantes tengan ocurrencias sobre organizar sus propias universidades. Aunque ya no existíamos en ese momento —cerramos en 2007—, recibimos esta carta diciéndonos que si alguna vez consideramos reabrir la Universidad Libre de Copenhagen sería ilegal. Todas nuestras pequeñas medidas se van acumulando.

DES SALAIRES POUR LES ÉTUDIANTS

Des salaires pour les étudiants a été écrit et publié anonymement par des activistes liés au journal *Zerowork* durant les grèves étudiantes du Massachusetts et de New York de l'automne 1975. Profondément influencés par l'analyse du capitalisme faite par la campagne pour le salaire ménager et liés à des luttes comme le Black Power, la resistance anticoloniale et les mouvements anti-guerre, les auteurs cherchaient à attaquer la fonction de l'université telle qu'elle avait été conçue par le capital et son État. La brochure débat des stratégies du mouvement étudiant de l'époque et dénonce le régime de travail non payé forcé imposé chaque jour à des millions d'étudiants. *Des salaires pour les étudiants* était un affront à une néolibéralisation de l'université qui n'en était alors qu'à ses débuts. Quarante ans plus tard, le très profitable business de l'éducation continue non seulement d'exploiter le travail non payé des étudiants mais désormais le leur fait payer. Aujourd'hui, alors que nous sommes embourbés jusqu'au coup dans la dette étudiante et que les étudiants à travers le monde refusent de continuer à collaborer, nous rendons de nouveau disponible ce texte « pour l'éducation contre l'éducation ».

Cette édition trilingue est édité par Jakob Jakobsen, María Berríos et Malav Kanuga, et contient une nouvelle introduction par George Caffentzis, Monty Neill et John Willshire-Carrera. Cette édition contient également la transcription d'une discussion collective organisée par Jakob Jakobsen, Malav Kanuga, Ayreen Anastas et Rene Gabri, qui faisait suite à une lecture publique de la brochure par George Caffentzis, Silvia Frederici, des étudiants de la Cooper Union et d'autres membres et amis de 16 Beaver (local alternatif de New York).

L'USINE DE DISCIPLINE MENTALE EN 1965

« C'EST LE MATIN. LE PRÉSENTATEUR MÉTÉO ANNONCE LA LEVÉE DU JOUR ET PLACE LE SOLEIL (OU LA PLUIE, LA NEIGE, LES NUAGES... OU CE QUI EST LE PLUS APPROPRIÉ) DANS LE CIEL. ET COMME UNE HORLOGE MÉCANIQUE, LES TIC-TACS DE LA TERRE RÉSONNENT AUTOUR DU SOLEIL. »

UNTEL APPARTIENT À L'UNITÉ 12 DE L'USINE DE DISCIPLINE MENTALE D'ELM CITY. IL EST NOTRE EXEMPLE DU JOUR. UNTEL EST ORDINAIRE, OU L'ÉTAIT, JUSQU'À CE QU'IL DÉRAPE. IL ÉTAIT ASSIS DANS NOTRE SALLE DES NÉCESSITÉS PHYSIQUES AVEC D'AUTRES PRODUCTIONS DE MASSES, SES COLLÈGUES, UN CRAYON DANS SA MAIN DROITE, UN PAPIER SUR SA TABLE, SON ESPRIT DÉDIÉ À SON TRA-VAIL, OCCUPÉ.

À PROPOS, QUELQUES PRÉCISIONS SUR LE CONTEXTE. LE PRÉTEXTE ORIGINAL DE L'EXISTENCE DE NOTRE SALLE DE NÉCESSITÉS PHYSIQUES ÉTAIT DE « PRODUIRE ET DISTRIBUER LA NOURRITURE QUI REMPLACERAIT NOS INSTRUCTIONS DISCIPLINAIRES PAR UNE STIMULATION PHYSIQUE ET UNE SEMI-SATISFACTION ». MAIS SON OBJET EST DÉSORMAIS DE SERVIR DE LIEU DE RÉUNION AUX UNTELS, QUI NE SONT PRO-GRAMMÉS À RIEN DE PLUS IMPORTANT. ICI NOUS LEUR APPRENONS L'OBÉISSANCE, UNE PART TRÈS, TRÈS IMPORTANTE DE LA DISCIPLINE MENTALE TOTALE.

Introduction à la présente édition

George Caffentzis, Monty Neill
et John Willshire-Carrera

Des salaires pour les étudiants fut publié anonymement par trois militants à l'automne 1975.

L'un était professeur assistant au Brooklyn College (qui fait partie du système universitaire new-yorkais) et les deux autres étaient étudiants en troisième cycle à l'université du Massachussetts, à Amherst.

Il n'est pas surprenant que la métropole new-yorkaise et l'État du Massachussetts soit les lieux d'origine d'une brochure sur la condition et les revendications des étudiants, puisque l'une et l'autre présentaient l'une des concentrations les plus élevées d'étudiants de troisième cycle aux États-Unis. New York et le Massachussetts furent pour les étudiants ce que Détroit fut pour les travailleurs de l'automobile.

La date de publication n'est pas surprenante si on regarde la conjoncture historique et théorique. Les auteurs participaient tous à un journal intitulé *Zerowork*. L'approche théorique de cette publication était une synthèse de la perspective opéraïste (venue d'Italie) et de la campagne pour le salaire au travail ménager initiée en 1972 par le Collectif féministe international. La perspective opéraïste prenait sa source dans les luttes des ouvriers de la ceinture industrielle s'étirant de Los Angeles à Turin, via Détroit, tandis que la campagne pour le salaire au travail ménager était issue des luttes des femmes demandant un salaire pour leurs activités domestiques, incluant ainsi la lutte pour les droits sociaux aux États-Unis.

À l'époque où *Des salaires pour les étudiants* fut écrit, la conscience théorique du fait que le « social » est un type particulier de lieu de production avait déjà émergé. Par le biais de ces convergences théoriques, le terrain était prêt à accueillir les germes d'une pensée nouvelle au sujet du travail étudiant. Le changement du rôle des universités impulsé par l'État avait un impact au-delà de ces influences théoriques et politiques.

C'était un axiome de la politique étatique des années 1950 et 1960 que les universités servaient à augmenter la productivité de la force de travail et la discipline sociale. Elles étaient des vecteurs d'ascension sociale et un moyen de subventionner des recherches qui génére-raient de nouvelles marchandises et méthodes de production. De fait, jusqu'à la fin des années 1960, capitalistes et travailleurs considéraient l'éducation comme un « bien commun ». Mais, à la suite de l'intense vague de luttes étudiantes des années 1960 — pour la liberté d'expression, les droits civiques, les droits des femmes et contre la conscription, la guerre du Vietnam et l'utilisation de la recherche universitaire à des fins militaires — il y eut un changement crucial dans l'attitude de la classe capitaliste vis-à-vis de l'éducation universitaire.

Sur ce point, la grève nationale des étudiants contre l'invasion du Cambodge et l'assassinat d'étudiants par des soldats à Kent et Jackson State marquèrent un tournant décisif. Le nouveau consensus capitaliste affirmait désormais que, au lieu de produire une force de travail qualifiée et fiable pour les usines, les bureaux et l'armée, les universités américaines (pourtant encore fraîchement purgées de leurs professeurs gauchistes par le maccarthysme des années 1950) engendraient des masses de diplômés anticapitalistes et anti-impérialistes. Et, comble de l'absurde, ces rebelles étaient subventionnés par des taxes locales et fédérales sur les entreprises. Il fallait que cela cesse. Dès les années 1970, les États et les entreprises demandèrent que les campus trop combatifs ne soient plus subventionnés et que les étudiants soient forcés de payer pour *leur propre éducation* — qui n'était plus vantée comme un bien commun.

Nous ne savions pas à l'époque comment nommer ce changement, mais nous étions conscients du tournant de ce qu'on allait bientôt appeler l'université « néolibérale », où l'éducation devient une marchandise que l'étudiant achète, un investissement qu'il/elle fait pour son avenir dans une institution elle-même modelée sur le schéma de l'entreprise.

La néolibéralisation de l'université commençait tout juste en 1975. *Des salaires pour les étudiants* décrivait ce tournant tout en en faisant la satire.

À l'époque où ce pamphlet était écrit, les auteurs participaient également aux évolutions qui se déroulaient au sein du mouvement étudiant. Après s'être engagés sur de nombreux problèmes « politiques », comme le racisme qui présidait aux admissions à l'université ou le recrutement militaire sur les campus, les étudiants commençaient à se sentir aussi concernés par les enjeux « économiques ».

Les manifestations contre la suspension des subventions aux universités, l'augmentation des frais de scolarité et la réduction des aides aux étudiants devinrent monnaie courante sur les campus. Rétrospectivement, on voit que cette nouvelle mobilisation étudiante essayait de contrer la néolibéralisation du système universitaire américain. *Des salaires pour les étudiants* proposait un langage, un vocabulaire à ce nouveau mouvement étudiant. Au lieu de décrire les étudiants comme des consommateurs ou des micro-entrepreneurs investissant dans leur avenir, la brochure les considérait comme des travailleurs. Et, contre la montée en flèche des frais de scolarité, elle appelait à un « salaire pour le travail scolaire ».

Des salaires pour les étudiants n'était pas seulement un ouvrage de réflexion ou un acte de provocation intellectuelle — même s'il était sûrement un peu des deux. Avec les camarades du cercle Zerowork, entre autres, les militants pour le salaire des étudiants faisaient du prosélytisme a travers tout le nord-est américain.

La première étape de ce travail politique fut d'attirer l'attention des étudiants sur cette perspective du salaire scolaire. Nous avons lancé l'idée dans les meetings de gauche. Nous avons écrit des tracts, distribué des autocollants, participé à des manifestations sur les campus et présenté nos thèses dans les cours de professeurs sympathisants. Nous rejetions les considérations propices aux divisions qui cherchaient à savoir « combien » ou « à qui » ces salaires devaient être payés. Le but était de créer des branches de la campagne pour le salaire étudiant dans les universités et construire un réseau, qui pourrait, pour commencer, changer le discours de la gauche (qui était dans certains endroits hostile à cette revendication) et de ce qui restait du mouvement étudiant.

La campagne pour le salaire étudiant prit comme modèle la campagne pour le salaire au travail ménager, qui atteignait dans le milieu des années 1970 son zénith organisationnel. Une grande partie de son travail d'organisation politique se construisait autour des attaques contre les femmes par le biais des aides sociales, justifiées à l'époque au nom de la crise budgétaire. La campagne nommait « aides sociales » le premier salaire au travail ménager.

La campagne pour le salaire étudiant s'inspira de cette idée d'expansion du salaire et chercha à l'appliquer à l'université. Tout comme la campagne pour le salaire au travail ménager analysait les « aides sociales » comme une première forme de salaire domestique, les activistes du salaire étudiant voyaient les différentes formes d'aides aux étudiants comme les prémices d'un salaire.

Nous rejoignions les manifestations et organisions des protestations contre les coupes de cette aide qu'ils décrivaient comme un salaire. Cette campagne, dans certains endroits, rassembla divers secteurs de la classe ouvrière, des « *welfare mothers* » et activistes communautaires jusqu'au étudiants de troisième cycle, dont beaucoup avaient pu accéder à l'université grâce aux luttes pour les droits civiques. Nous comprenions que même si la revendication d'un salaire étudiant, comme beaucoup de luttes pour l'augmentation des salaires, n'était pas en soi révolutionnaire, mettre fin au travail « non salarié » sous toutes ses formes déstabiliserait, voire renverserait, le système capitaliste puisque ce secteur générait énormément de plus-value.

En tant que militants, nous comprenions aussi qu'être payés pour nos études nous fournirait de nouvelles armes pour refuser le travail quotidien imposé par le capital, notamment celui nécessaire au travail scolaire. Ce travail nous privait du temps pour penser, créer et prendre soin les uns des autres. Comme ceux qui militaient pour le salaire au travail ménager, nous comprenions qu'être payés pour étudier nous donnerait au bout du compte un plus grand pouvoir pour refuser le travail imposé par le capital.

Il est clair, rétrospectivement, que le capital éta-
sunien et son État comprenaient que l'expansion
du salaire, prônée par les campagnes autour du
travail ménager et des étudiants, était une me-
nace politique pour le système. Ce n'est pas un
hasard si nombre de réformes néolibérales de
ces trente dernières années ont été des attaques
contre les droits sociaux et le libre accès à l'éducation universitaire ; et que ces attaques ont été
menées tout autant par les républicains que par
les démocrates, en parallèle des coupes dans les
salaires et les avantages des salariés.

Le salaire étudiant, comme revendication,
a malheureusement surgi au moment où
les stratèges aux États-Unis étaient en train
d'abandonner la politique keynésienne de
subsomption des luttes salariales dans le plan
de développement du capital. Et, au lieu d'un
salaire étudiant, il y eut une énorme augmentation des frais de scolarité (+ 500% entre
1985 et aujourd'hui). Au final, l'étudiant en-
detté moyen a désormais une dette de près de
30 000 dollars et la totalité de la dette étudiante
dépasse 1,1 trillion de dollars. Au lieu d'obtenir
le salaire scolaire, les étudiants aux États-Unis
ont payé pour travailler dans les universités et
se préparer pour leur future exploitation.

Il est bien sûr gratifiant de voir, quarante ans après sa publication, un intérêt renouvelé pour ce qui peut apparaître comme une note de bas de page à contre-courant dans la réforme néolibérale de l'université. De quel usage peut être cette brochure aujourd'hui pour un mouvement étudiant de nouveau mobilisé, du Chili au Québec en passant par de nombreuses villes américaines ? Les mouvements eux-mêmes doivent le décider. La façon dont la nouvelle génération réagira à ce texte nous fournira une intéressante leçon politique.

D'ores et déjà, nous pouvons voir que *Des salaires pour les étudiants* peut servir un objectif. En montrant que les étudiants sont des travailleurs et que ce qu'ils font dans les universités n'est pas consommer une marchandise nommé « éducation », le texte renforce la lutte contre la dette étudiante. Il établit que ce ne sont pas les étudiants qui doivent aux universités, au gouvernement et aux banques une large somme d'argent. Ce sont ces institutions qui devraient payer les étudiants alors qu'ils prospèrent sur leur travail non payé. Dans la période actuelle, alors que les politiciens proposent des solutions néolibérales à la crise créée par la dette étudiante, comme classer les universités pour que les étudiants deviennent des « consommateurs éclairés sur le marché de l'éducation », *Des sa-laires pour les étudiants* répond que les étudiants sont des travailleurs dont l'exploitation non sa-lariée doit être payée.

New York, 2015

Des salaires pour les étudiants
(Un pamphlet sous la forme d'un livre bleu, 1975)

Les étudiants « Des salaires pour les étudiants »

L'usine de discipline mentale en 1965

« C'est le matin. Le présentateur météo annonce que le jour s'est levé (ou la pluie, la neige, les nuages . . . c'est selon) dans le ciel. Et comme une horloge mécanique, la Terre refait le tour du Soleil en tic-tac réguliers. »

Untel appartient à l'unité 12 de l'usine de discipline mentale d'Elm City. Il est Notre Exemple du jour. Untel est ordinaire, ou l'était, jusqu'à ce qu'il Dérape. Il était assis dans Notre salle des besoins corporels avec d'autres produits en série, ses collègues, un crayon dans la main droite, un papier sur la table, l'esprit au travail, occupé.

Quelques précisions sur le contexte, d'ailleurs. Le prétexte à l'origine de Notre salle des besoins corporels était de produire et distribuer une nourriture qui bonifierait Nos enseignements disciplinaires par une récompense physique et une satisfaction partielle. Mais elle sert maintenant de lieu de rassemblement aux Untels, qui n'ont rien de plus important à l'agenda. Ici on leur apprend l'obéissance, *une part très, très importante de la discipline mentale générale.*

Mais revenons à l'Untel. Il allait Bien jusqu'à ce qu'il ait l'audace de se lever, d'aller directement à Notre fontaine d'eau et d'avaler deux énormes gorgées, emplissant complètement sa bouche et tarissant ainsi sa soif à nos dépens.

Voyons, Vous avez tous été éduqués pour vous rendre compte que ce n'est pas la raison d'être de Nos fontaines d'eau. Vous avez été programmés pour comprendre qu'elles servent de tentation disciplinaire et participent en cela, et en cela uniquement, à Notre Plan. Il vous faut maîtriser votre soif, contrairement à Untel. Il est mauvais, mauvais, mauvais. Un de Nos superviseurs a dû le faire escorter jusqu'au chirurgien, qui lui a immédiatement cousu les lèvres.

Certains d'entre Nous pensons que la punition d'Untel a été trop peu sévère pour un acte de désobéissance aussi honteux. Mais nous croyons encore à la clémence. Un Principe est un Principe, mais que vaut un principe si nous ignorons l'humain ?

Étudiez le sens de ceci pour le cours de demain.

(Écrit dans un lycée par un étudiant du secondaire.)

Qu'est-ce que le travail scolaire ?

Aller à l'école, être un étudiant, c'est un travail. On le nomme travail scolaire, bien qu'il ne soit pas considéré usuellement comme un vrai travail puisque l'on ne reçoit aucun salaire pour l'accomplir. Cela ne veut pas dire que le travail scolaire n'est pas un travail, mais plutôt qu'ils nous ont appris à croire que l'on ne travaille <u>vraiment</u> que lorsqu'on perçoit un salaire.

Le travail scolaire se compose d'une grande diversité de tâches d'intensités variées, combinant travail qualifié et non qualifié. Par exemple : il nous faut apprendre à rester en classe, calmement assis pour de longs moments sans déranger. Il nous faut écouter attentivement et tenter de mémoriser ce qui nous est présenté. Il nous faut obéir aux professeurs. À l'occasion, nous acquérons quelques compétences techniques qui nous rendent plus productifs lorsque nous travaillons hors de l'école à des boulots qui les exigent. La majeure partie de notre temps, toutefois, nous le passons à exercer quantités de travaux non qualifiés.

La caractéristique partagée par l'ensemble des tâches spécifiques requises par le travail scolaire est la Discipline — c'est-à-dire, le travail forcé. Parfois on nous discipline, ce qui veut dire que les autres (des professeurs, des directeurs et des inspecteurs) nous forcent à travailler. D'autres fois nous nous autodisciplinons, ce qui veut dire que nous nous forçons nous-mêmes au travail scolaire. Il n'est pas étonnant que les différentes catégories de travail scolaire aient été communément nommées « Disciplines ».

Il est évidemment moins cher et plus avantageux pour le Capital que nous nous disciplinions nous-mêmes. Cela lui évite d'avoir à payer pour des professeurs, directeurs, et gardiens qui, étant des travailleurs salariés, doivent être rémunérés. En tant qu'étudiants auto-disciplinés, nous accomplissons la double-tâche d'effectuer le travail scolaire et de nous obliger à le faire. Voilà pourquoi les directeurs d'école accordent autant d'attention aux aspects auto-disciplinaires de l'école, tout en tentant de garder les coûts de la discipline au minimum.

Comme toutes les institutions capitalistes, les écoles sont des usines. Les notes et les examens sont des manières de mesurer notre productivité à l'intérieur de l'école-usine. On ne nous forme pas seulement à atteindre notre future « position sociale », on nous programme également à prendre la « place appropriée » pour nous. L'école-usine est un échelon essentiel dans le processus de sélection qui destinera certains à balayer les rues et d'autres à superviser ceux qui balaient.

Le travail scolaire peut aussi inclure un type de connaissance que les étudiants trouvent utile. Cependant, cet aspect est strictement subordonné à l'intérêt le plus immédiat du Capital : la discipline de la classe ouvrière. Parce qu'au final, quel bénéfice y a-t-il pour le Capital qu'un ingénieur parle chinois et puisse résoudre des équations différentielles s'il ne se présente jamais au travail ?

Pourquoi le travail scolaire ?

La plupart des économistes sont d'accord : « Le travail scolaire est autant un bien de consommation qu'un investissement. » Ainsi, leur réponse à la question de la raison d'être du travail scolaire est que les études possèdent cette merveilleuse double-qualité. Vous investissez en vous de telle façon que vous pouvez vous attendre à obtenir une rémunération élevée en travaillant, et en plus c'est amusant ! Nous sommes bien loin des jours où investir signifiait s'abstenir, mais peut-on vraiment prendre ces foutaises au sérieux ?

Considérons, comme les économistes, qu'un bien de consommation est quelque chose dont on peut profiter, qui nous apporte joie et satisfaction, alors tous ceux qui voient en l'école un « bien » de consommation doivent plaisanter. La pression constante pour terminer les tâches, le rouleau compresseur des horaires, les absurdes nuits blanches passées à étudier pour des examens, et tous les autres mécanismes d'auto-discipline tuent dans l'oeuf toute possibilité d'amusement. C'est comme dire qu'aller en prison est un bien de consommation, parce qu'il est réjouissant d'en sortir !

Certains diront que l'on peut avoir un peu de plaisir à aller à l'école ; bien sûr, mais ce n'est pas dans l'éducation qu'on le trouve. Au contraire, c'est la lutte contre cette éducation qui est source de jouissance. Ce sont les expéditions que l'on entreprend pour s'échapper des salles de classe, les histoires d'amour qui sont si divertissantes, les conversations interminables dans les bars, les manifestations qui ferment l'école, les livres qui n'étaient pas à lire et les livres au programme, lus au mauvais moment : tout ce que nous faisons pour ne pas être éduqués. Ainsi, du point de vue de la consommation, la conclusion est à l'exact opposé de celles des économistes.

Qu'en est-il du côté de « l'investissement » ? Tout au long des années 1960, professeurs d'économie, banquiers, « conseillers » s'accordaient : l'école était un investissement personnel avantageux. Il s'agissait de faire de soi une petite entreprise, un General Motors en miniature, afin d'investir dans sa propre personne en allant à l'école, de la même manière qu'une entreprise achète une machine afin d'augmenter ses bénéfices, en se basant sur le principe suivant : il faut dépenser de l'argent (investir) pour faire de l'argent. Celui qui parvenait à rassembler l'argent (et le courage) d'aller à l'école — en obtenant un prêt, un second boulot, ou en faisant payer ses parents — pouvait s'attendre à faire fructifier cet argent, puisque l'augmentation de son niveau d'éducation lui permettrait d'obtenir un boulot mieux payé à l'avenir. À l'apogée de ce qu'ils appelaient alors la « révolution du capital humain », les économistes les plus réputés considéraient que l'on obtenait un meilleur retour en investissant dans son éducation que dans des actions de GM. Un capitalisme pour la classe ouvrière — vengeance en sus !

En plus du caractère un peu répugnant de ce « point de vue de l'investisseur » — après tout, si je suis une entreprise, une partie de moi sera un travailleur et l'autre, le patron qui dirige ce travailleur — on peut s'interroger pour savoir s'il est bien vrai que l'on fait plus d'argent à long terme en allant à l'école. Dans les années 1960, tout le monde nous l'assurait, mais en ces années 1970, « dominées par la crise », on n'est plus sûrs de rien. Les autorités disent maintenant que leurs analyses étaient erronées, qu'il n'y a pas de retour garanti pour un tel investissement dans soi-même. Il fallait s'y attendre — nous ne sommes plus d'aussi bons générateurs de profit que GM ! Au mieux, elles entrevoient maintenant une augmentation hypothétique de ce qu'elles nomment le revenu « psychique », puisqu'une meilleure éducation permet de mettre la main sur un « meilleur » boulot — bien que ce ne soit pas en terme de salaire. Mais même cela n'est pas garanti, d'autant moins que tous les « bons » boulots « décents » sont en passe de devenir incertains, plus ardus, voire dangereux — enseigner, par exemple. Il semblerait que les étudiants soient une erreur de planification.

Les professeurs « socialistes » et les étudiants « révolutionnaires » sont devenus les plus ardents défenseurs de l'université publique contre les « coupes budgétaires » et autres mesures du même acabit. Pourquoi ? On peut le résumer comme suit : l'éducation permet à chacun d'analyser plus finement sa situation sociale — en un mot, l'éducation rend plus conscient. Puisque les universités publiques ouvrent la voie au développement d'une classe ouvrière hautement éduquée, elles permettent à la classe ouvrière d'acquérir une conscience de classe ; de plus, une classe ouvrière plus consciente portera moins d'attention aux simples revendications « économiques » — plus d'argent pour moins de travail — et s'attellera plutôt à la tâche politique qu'est la « construction du socialisme ». Cette logique fournit à la Gauche à la fois une explication de la crise universitaire — le capital a peur de cette classe ouvrière très conscientisée que l'université commencerait à engendrer — et une revendication : pas moins, mais plus de travail scolaire ! C'est donc au nom de la conscience politique et du socialisme que ces gauchistes intensifient le travail scolaire (qui n'est rien d'autre qu'un travail sans salaire) et désapprouvent les revendications étudiantes prônant l'inverse, y voyant une régression capitaliste. Alors même que toutes les justifications habituelles du travail gratuit effectué à l'école sont révélées au grand jour, la Gauche s'empare du moment comme d'une occasion de sortir la classe ouvrière de son sommeil « matérialiste » et de la mener vers sa mission la plus élevée : la construction de la société socialiste.

Mais la Gauche s'embourbe dans cette vieille question posée à d'anciens esprits éclairés de la classe ouvrière : qui éduquera les éducateurs ? Puisque la Gauche ne part pas de ce qui est évident — le travail scolaire est un travail non payé — tous ses efforts conduisent à plus de travail non payé pour le capital et à plus d'exploitation. Toutes ses tentatives d'élever la conscience de classe continuent de fermer les yeux au contrôle qu'exerce le capital sur son propre terrain. Ainsi, la Gauche finit par soutenir systématiquement les efforts du capital en vue d'intensifier le travail, en rationalisant et disciplinant la classe ouvrière. La « construction du socialisme » devient un simple mécanisme supplémentaire pour extraire davantage de travail gratuit au service du capital.

Ainsi, la justification du caractère gratuit du travail scolaire par le Capital et la Gauche s'écroule tout simplement.

Les étudiants sont des travailleurs non payés

Les étudiants appartiennent à la classe ouvrière. Plus précisément, nous appartenons à cette partie de la classe ouvrière qui n'est pas salariée (non payée). Notre absence de rémunération nous condamne à vivre pauvres, dépendants et surchargés de travail. Mais, pire que tout, elle nous prive du pouvoir que le salaire confère dans notre rapport de force avec le capital.

Sans salaire, nous sommes condamnés à nous contenter de peu. Nous devons survivre avec ce que d'aucuns ne pourraient tolérer. Les seuls logements que nous pouvons nous

permettre de louer sont insalubres et sur-
peuplés. La nourriture que nous mangeons,
que nous devons manger, est la nourriture
industrielle insipide des marques les moins
chères. Nos habits et nos loisirs sont stan-
dardisés et fades. Nous vivons à l'évidence
dans la pauvreté.

Puisque nous sommes généralement non
payés et que nous devons tout de même
vivre, il nous faut trouver de l'argent ailleurs —
en étant dépendant de quelqu'un qui reçoit,
lui, un salaire. Pour certains étudiants, les dé-
penses nécessaires à la survie ainsi que les frais
de scolarité sont assumés, au moins en partie,
par un parent attentionné. Mais la relation de
dépendance à nos parents et autres bienfai-
teurs qui découle de notre statut d'étudiants
non payés nous laisse impuissants. De plus,
lorsqu'une famille entière se sacrifie — la
mère prend un deuxième travail et le père
s'épuise — pour payer les frais scolaires, nos
parents perdent des forces pour leur propre
lutte contre le travail tandis que la pression
pour que nous acceptions le travail scolaire
s'accentue. Même si nous travaillons autant
que les salariés, notre situation nous rend dépendants d'eux ; en effet, à l'exception de
ces étudiants qui reçoivent un salaire (dans
l'armée, dans la prison « avant-gardiste » de
Lompoc en Californie, dans les programmes
de formation privée des grandes entreprises,

dans la formation « Manpower »), la plupart des étudiants ne touchent aucun salaire pour leur travail scolaire.

Pour ceux d'entre nous qui ne reçoivent aucune aide, ne pas avoir de salaire signifie devoir travailler en dehors de l'école. Et, comme le marché du travail est saturé d'étudiants à la recherche de ce type d'emplois, le capital impose les salaires les plus bas et engendre des profits à la sueur de nos fronts. En conséquence, nous travaillons encore plus, et nous cumulons les emplois. Puisque notre travail scolaire n'est pas payé, nous travaillons durant la majorité des soi-disant vacances d'été. Lorsque nous prenons un peu de vacances, nous n'avons de toutes façons pas les moyens d'en profiter. L'absurdité de cette situation est d'autant plus amplifiée par les standards de productivité très élevés qui nous sont constamment imposés en tant qu'étudiants (les examens, les QCM, les dissertations, etc.) et par le fait qu'on nous programme à nous en imposer encore plus à nous-mêmes (crédits scolaires hors programme, lectures et réflexions supplémentaires pour nos cours — pas pour nous –, stages en entreprise, soutien scolaire, etc.). D'un côté, nous devons travailler pour rien et, de l'autre, nous devons travailler pour presque rien. Bien sûr, on nous dit que l'avenir nous vaudra tous ces efforts. On nous dit qu'un travail passionnant nous attend, avec un gros salaire et une secrétaire en bonus. Nous ne travaillons pas gratuitement en vain. Mais nous savons bien, avant de sortir de cette usine en sautillant de joie, qu'il n'y a pour nous d'autres perspectives que celle d'un boulot déprimant de réceptionniste à l'hôtel Holiday Inn du coin ou, au mieux, de secrétaire en notre lieu de travail précédent, l'université.

En réalité, la situation actuelle nous montre que certains étudiants commencent à être payés pour leur travail scolaire :

• Forces armées : le ROTC (Reserve Officers Training Corps) paye 100 $ par mois plus les frais de scolarité ;
• certaines entreprises payent leurs employés lorsqu'ils suivent des cours du soir ou qu'ils poursuivent leurs études afin obtenir un diplôme plus élevé ;
• la prison de Lompoc paye des prisonniers pour leur travail scolaire à l'université de Californie ;
• les clients de la « Formation Manpower » touchent des bourses pendant leur formation ;
• les bénéficiaires de la sécurité sociale ;
• les étudiants boursiers (BEOG)
• les vétérans de la guerre du Vietnam.

Des salaires pour les étudiants

Nous en avons assez de travailler gratuitement.

Nous exigeons immédiatement de l'argent pour notre travail scolaire.

Nous devons obliger le capital, qui tire profit de notre travail, à payer pour notre travail scolaire. Alors seulement nous ne dépendrons plus, pour notre survie, des aides financières, de nos parents, d'un deuxième ou d'un troisième emploi, ou encore de celui que nous occupons durant les vacances d'été. Nous gagnons déjà un salaire ; il nous faut maintenant le toucher. Voilà notre seul moyen de nous saisir d'un plus grand pouvoir dans nos négociations avec le capital.

Nous pouvons faire beaucoup avec cet argent. Premièrement, nous n'aurons pas à travailler autant, puisque le « besoin de travailler » à d'autres emplois disparaîtra. Deuxièmement, nous jouirons immédiatement d'un niveau de vie plus élevé puisque nous aurons plus d'argent à dépenser dans notre temps libre. Enfin, nous ferons augmenter le salaire moyen pour l'ensemble des secteurs présentement affectés par la présence des travailleurs sous payés que nous sommes.

En prenant congé de notre travail scolaire afin d'exiger des salaires pour les étudiants, nous pensons et agissons contre le travail que nous accomplissons. Cela nous met aussi dans une meilleure position pour obtenir cet argent.

QU'ON EN FINISSE AVEC
LE TRAVAIL SCOLAIRE NON PAYÉ !

Les étudiants
« Des salaires pour les étudiants »

Des salaires aux dettes,
des étudiants aux emprunteurs,
de la vie à . . .*

16 Beaver, New York
dimanche le 3 mars 2013

René Gabri : Nous avons pensé à un format simple pour cette soirée. L'idée est que Jakob Jakobsen se présente et nous parle un peu du travail qui l'occupe depuis un certain temps, de fait depuis que nous le connaissons, c'est-à-dire environ dix ans, ce qui l'a amené à *Des salaires pour les étudiants*, ainsi que les questions qu'il se pose à ce sujet ; et peut-être George Caffentzis et Silvia Federici pourront parler un peu et répondre à quelques unes de ces questions, puis nous poserons nous-mêmes nos propres questions.

---

* Il s'agit de la transcription d'une conversation qui s'est tenue au 16 Beaver le dimanche 3 mars 2013. La discussion a duré deux heures et demi et a été éditée du fait de sa longueur. Certaines répétitions ou propos annexes n'ont pas été reproduits mais la plupart des choses qui se sont dites se trouvent dans cette retranscription.

La discussion a été enregistré avec l'accord des personnes présentes et les éditeurs ont essayé de contacter tous ceux dont les interventions sont retranscrites ici. Néanmoins comme il s'agissait d'un événement public, il n'a pas été possible d'identifier tous les locuteurs d'où l'apparition dans le texte d'« intervenants inconnus ».

Jakob Jakobsen : Merci. En fait, nous avons discuté de l'organisation de cette présentation de nombreuses fois, mais de façon approximative. Et nous n'étions pas d'accord, ce qui est un bon point de départ pour une discussion. J'espère donc que ce sera plus une soirée d'échanges qu'une simple présentation. Nous espérons que les gens poseront des questions et interviendront comme ils le souhaitent.

RG : Et nous nous interromprons.

JJ : Ce qui, selon moi, nous réunit ce soir est ce petit livre *Des salaires pour les étudiants*, que j'ai trouvé au salon du livre anarchiste de Londres il y a quelques années. Comme je connaissais George et Silvia, j'ai écrit à cette dernière pour lui demander si elle savait quoi que ce soit à ce sujet et elle m'a dit : « Oui, bien sûr, c'est George. »

Je le lui ai demandé car *Des salaires pour les étudiants* se rapproche du travail de Silvia et je me doutais qu'elle en savait quelque chose. Si j'ai choisi de parler de ce pamphlet — pour me présenter un peu — c'est que je fais des recherches sur l'histoire de l'éducation et des luttes qui l'entourent depuis un certain temps. J'ai travaillé à un programme d'archivage pour un projet de recherche sur l'anti-université de Londres, une université expérimentale née en

1968, qui a duré environ trois ans — on ne peut pas dater précisément la fin de son activité, ce qui indique un peu son caractère expérimental. Les étudiants dirigeaient cette structure autogérée. C'est ce qui a fait que cette anti-institution s'est peu à peu désinstitutionnalisée et a disparu dans la structure sociale de Londres et du monde. Si je pense qu'il est important de parler de ces choses, c'est qu'on peut connecter les luttes dans le temps — *Des salaires pour les étudiants* date de 1975 — et dans l'espace. Je vis à Londres et j'y suis les luttes sur l'éducation. J'étais très intéressé de venir ici pour parler avec George, Silvia et vous tous pour m'informer sur ce qui se passe à New York. J'espérais surtout venir écouter et non parler. Ce que je suggère maintenant c'est que nous lisions la brochure ensemble.

Malav Kanuga : Chacun à notre tour ?

JJ : Oui.

(*Lecture collective de* Des salaires pour les étudiants)

JJ : Je vais revenir vers toi George, mais j'aimerais d'abord commencer avec une question pour toi Silvia. Voir les études comme un travail dans le cadre de l'économie capitaliste, comme un travail non-payé, est — du moins pour moi — une idée intéressante.

Bien sûr, elle est à rapprocher de tes luttes et de ton travail sur la relation entre travail produc- tif et reproductif. Si le travail productif est le travail à l'usine, qui est reconnu et couplé à un salaire, le travail reproductif est celui qui sou- tient le travail productif, que ce soit en terme de travail ménager, domestique ou d'études. La question intéressante est celle de la relation entre travail productif et reproductif. Donc, j'aimerais bien te demander, Silvia, si tu pourrais réfléchir à cette conception des études comme du travail non payé au sein de la production capitaliste.

Silvia Federici : C'était une conséquence logique de la conceptualisation du travail domestique comme faisant partie d'un large spectre d'activi- tés par lesquelles la force de travail est produite. C'était réaliser qu'il y a une ligne de montage qui court, non pas seulement à travers l'usine mais à travers toute la société — les foyers, les écoles — et qui produit des ouvriers, qui à leur tour produisent des marchandises et des profits. Redéfinir les activités domestiques comme un travail qui produit la force de travail fournissait un nouveau point de vue sur la fonction de l'éducation. L'école est la continuation du foyer, elle entraîne et discipline de futurs travailleurs. Discipliner les nouvelles générations est aussi un aspect important du travail domestique. C'est ce qui le rend si difficile. Ce n'est pas seulement l'effort physique, mais le fait que ça suppose une lutte constante, avoir à dire « non » et « tu ne dois pas faire ça ». L'auto-discipline peut être nécessaire indépendamment de l'organisation capitaliste du travail ; mais dans la plupart des cas, la discipline que nous enseignons à nos enfants est dictée par nos attentes vis-à-vis de leur insertion dans le marché du travail. C'est le travail des pères et des mères de former nos désirs, de s'assurer que nous correspondrons aux attentes du marché du travail.

C'était très important pour les femmes et le mouvement féministe de réaliser cela, car il y avait toujours un sentiment très lourd de culpabilité associé à l'idée de lutter contre le travail domestique. Son refus entraînait un tel sentiment de culpabilité car les femmes avaient l'impression de détruire le bien-être de leurs familles, le bien-être de gens dont elles étaient sensées s'occuper. Donc, être capable d'identifier et de démêler ces aspects du travail domestique qui visent particulièrement à la production d'un travailleur, la production d'une personne qui est destinée à être exploitée, était un processus libérateur. Nous avons réalisé que nous pouvions soit reproduire des gens pour la lutte ou les reproduire pour le marché du travail. Bien sûr, la ligne de séparation n'est pas toujours aussi claire. Mais c'était libérateur, car cela permettait de penser que la lutte contre le travail ménager n'a pas à être une lutte contre les personnes auxquelles nous tenons.

Nous avons ensuite étendu cette approche au travail scolaire. Une grande partie de celui-ci, que l'on étudie le français ou les mathématiques, consiste à apprendre à être discipliné. C'est la première chose que l'on attend de nous. La campagne pour le salaire au travail ménager nous permettait de voir que l'école nous prépare au travail et que nous y allons pour obtenir un diplôme, pas pour le plaisir d'étudier. Cela nous permettait de montrer la façon dont l'organisation de l'école est dictée par les besoins du marché du travail. Et enfin, cela nous donnait un aperçu des conséquences de la dépendance économique des étudiants. Si tu ne gagnes pas un salaire, tu dépends alors de ceux qui payent pour toi. Ce rapport de dépendance suppose des relations de pouvoir. Certaines personnes disent : « Si ton mari gagne un salaire, c'est donc que tu as aussi de l'argent. » Mais ce n'est pas vrai. Quelque soit la somme qu'on te donne, il faut que tu sois reconnaissante. Ce n'est pas quelque chose auquel tu as droit. C'est la même chose avec les étudiants. Quand tu gagnes un salaire avec ton travail, tu as une certaine autonomie, au moins par rapport à la famille et la communauté. Mais si tu travailles pour rien, alors tu dépends des autres. De plus, quand tu es socialement défini comme travailleur non salarié, comme le sont les étudiants et les travailleurs domestiques, tu es aussi destiné à devenir du travail bon marché. La condition du travailleur domestique et celle de l'étudiant sont très similaires. Clairement, les gens du collectif Zerowork qui ont écrit *Des salaires pour les étudiants* étaient inspirés par la campagne pour le salaire au travail ménager.

George Caffentzis : Oui.

SF : Ce qui est aussi surprenant, c'est à quel point la brochure est encore actuelle. Particulièrement dans la première partie, on voit que nous nous opposions déjà à l'idéologie néolibérale. Dès les années 1970, les signes avant-coureur de la conception néolibérale de l'éducation comme un investissement étaient visibles, même s'ils ne pouvaient l'imposer avant d'avoir démantelé l'État social, l'investissement de l'État dans l'éducation et d'autres formes de reproduction.

JJ : C'était écrit . . .

SF : . . . en 1975, des années avant le plein déploiement du néolibéralisme, les premiers présages étaient déjà là. Particulièrement à New York où ils commençaient à nous dire : « Nous ne vous devons pas une éducation, vous devez payer pour l'avoir. »

JJ : Peut-être que des gens ici en savent plus, mais j'ai compris que c'est en 1976 que l'université de New York est devenue payante. En 1975, quand le texte a été publié, c'était encore une université gratuite. Mais, George, ce qui a particulièrement retenu mon attention dans le texte, c'est la perspective d'une « éducation contre l'éducation ». Il y a aujourd'hui beaucoup de luttes dans les facs contre les coupes budgétaires et la privatisation, pour la préservation de l'institution. Mais là, justement, tu reproches à la gauche de se cramponner à un modèle institutionnel qui est basiquement disciplinaire, un modèle qui forme des étudiants pour qu'ils deviennent des travailleurs obéissants. C'est une perspective qu'on pourrait qualifier d'« anarchiste », dont je n'ai pas vu d'équivalent récemment. Les gens tendent à s'accrocher à ces institutions disciplinaires plutôt que de s'y soustraire ou de les critiquer radicalement. Il n'y a pas beaucoup d'auto-organisation en dehors des institutions, cherchant à développer « l'éducation contre l'éducation » que tu suggérais. Peut-être peux-tu nous en dire un peu plus sur comment on en est arrivés là ?

GC : Le texte *Des salaires pour les étudiants* a été écrit en 1975 au moment où le premier numéro de *Zerowork* était achevé. Il a été rédigé par trois personnes : moi-même et deux autres, John Willshire-Carrera et Leoncio Schaedel, qui étaient étudiants au département d'économie de l'université du Massachusetts. Nous étions tous impliqués dans un projet politique qui faisait converger ce que nous considérions comme deux révolutions politiques et conceptuelles. La première était la théorie du salaire au travail ménager, qui rendait visible tout l'univers du travail non payé. Cela avait eu un profond impact sur tous ceux qui s'étaient formés à l'école d'un marxisme pour lequel le travail salarié était à la base de la société capitaliste et la classe ouvrière salariée l'élément moteur du dépassement du capitalisme. (*Un camion de ramassage des ordures commence son travail à l'extérieur. GC doit élever sa voix pour continuer.*) Cela amenait une façon complètement nouvelle d'envisager la nature du travail. La seconde révolution politique et conceptuelle (*partiellement inaudible*) plaçait au centre de la lutte des classes le refus du travail.

Selon cette perspective, la lutte des classes trouvait sa source dans le rejet et non dans l'identification au travail. Cette identification a été pendant longtemps le pilier des politiques de gauche et marxistes. Elle était associée à l'association de l'éducation et de libération. Cette brochure met en cause cette perspective et soutient que ce qui importe est notre refus de donner au capital et de nous identifier à notre travail.

SF : De même, la gauche disait aux femmes que prendre un travail était la voie vers l'émancipation : « Prends un travail, rejoins le syndicat, rejoins la lutte des classes. C'est comme cela que tu gagneras du pouvoir social et que tu appartiendras à la classe ouvrière. »

GC : Oui. Il est évident que, quarante ans après, j'ai quelques critiques à faire sur cette brochure. Il faut réaliser que l'écriture, l'impression et la distribution de ce texte participaient d'une campagne politique. Nous avons commencé avec un petit groupe de gens et nous avons fini avec un petit groupe de gens (*rires*). Mais entre-temps, nous avons passé plusieurs années à faire de l'agitation autour de cette revendication. Nous participions aux luttes contre la mise en place de frais de scolarité à l'université de New-York en 1976. J'étais moi-même très en colère contre le syndicat des professeurs de l'université qui négociait avec la direction à ce sujet. Je critiquais l'action du syndicat et la gauche en général, qui voyait l'université comme un moyen d'émancipation. Il présentait l'université-usine comme un lieu de libération, alors que nous disions qu'il était au contraire temps de se libérer de ces usines, de les refuser.

J'ai particulièrement repensé à cette brochure récemment, à l'occasion de mon activité au sein des campagnes Occupy Student Debt et Strike Debt. Nous nous battions pour des salaires étudiants dans les années 1970 et maintenant nous essayons d'échapper à un servage par la dette; ces quarante dernières années, les étudiants se sont endettés de façon faramineuse pour pouvoir être exploités. Ce n'est pas arrivé par accident. Déjà à la fin des années 1960 et au début des années 1970, les stratèges du capital, Gary Becker par exemple, travaillaient sur un projet d'université néolibérale avant même que ce terme « néolibéralisme » ait trouvé son sens actuel. C'est décrit dans *Des salaires pour les étudiants* et c'est l'une des contributions de cette brochure à la compréhension du présent. Ce qui s'est passé ces quarante dernières années n'est que le résultat de cette stratégie néolibérale et ce jusqu'à sa sinistre conclusion — qui illustre effectivement la malédiction proférée par Thomas Carlyle contre l'économie, cette « science sinistre ». Quand je regarde cette assistance, je suis sûr que je vois des gens qui sont confrontés à un futur lugubre de remboursements et de défauts de paiement *ad infinitum*. C'est le genre de résultat que nous espérions empêcher et même renverser à l'époque où nous écrivions *Des salaires pour les étudiants*. Mais les courants à l'œuvre étaient trop forts.

SF : Désormais on doit payer pour être exploité. Il faut payer pour avoir le privilège d'être formé en vue d'une exploitation future. C'est une double exploitation.

GC : Oui, c'est de la folie.

JJ : Pour continuer sur cette critique de l'institution éducative simplement vue comme une machine à discipliner : puisque l'éducation ne peut pas être un instrument de libération, vous ne souscriviez pas à l'idée qu'elle est un moyen d'élévation sociale pour la classe ouvrière ou de développement de la conscience. Votre critique du système éducatif était générale, et vous n'étiez pas pragmatiques à propos des gains éventuels de l'éducation.

GC : À ce moment-là, nous théorisions le fait que le plus important était le pouvoir et pas la conscience. Nous pensions que ce qui était crucial, c'était de changer les relations de pouvoir qui, selon nous, se fondaient sur le salaire. L'argument que nous développions était une vraie transformation de l'université supposait une aptitude accrue des étudiants à organiser leur vie et à rompre avec le travail de discipline qui était crucial à l'éducation capitaliste. C'était la logique, à la fois implicite et explicite, du texte. Donc tu as raison, dans ce sens, c'est une critique de l'éducation.

JJ : Si on rapproche cela de ce qui arrive aujourd'hui avec la dette et le servage par la dette, on peut aussi analyser la dette comme un dispositif disciplinaire.

GC : Plutôt deux fois qu'une !

SF : Et les notes ! On devrait écrire un livre sur la nuit de notation du gauchiste ! La nuit dégradante (*jeux de mots en anglais sur « grade », qui signifie note*) du professeur gauchiste. J'ai eu tant de conversations à ce sujet avec des collègues de gauche . . .

RG : La nuit dégradante du gauchiste ?

SF : Oui. Est-ce que quelqu'un comprend de quoi je parle ?

Ayrenn Anastas : Oui. Quand il faut distribuer les notes avant le lendemain . . .

SF : Oui. Demain, il faut que vous ayez noté tous vos étudiants, mais vous êtes un professeur éclairé et vous savez, bien sûr, ce que la notation signifie. Vous savez que c'est l'essence même du système de classes. Néanmoins, vous considérez *tellement* l'éducation comme élévatrice et potentiellement révolutionnaire — vos cours portent peut-être sur la pensée de Marx — que vous devez vous assurer que vos étudiants prennent au sérieux ce que vous enseignez. Donc il faut que vous décidiez si c'est un B ou un B- ou un C+. Ou encore C- voire un D. Les gens passent des nuits entières à prendre ce genre de décisions, en voulant être juste avec leurs étudiants mais en faisant en général abstraction du contexte dans lequel ces décisions sont prises, c'est-à-dire là où on vous demande de faire une sélection, la plupart du temps sur une base de classe. C'est un des moments où la vérité surgit à la surface des choses. À la fin du semestre sur Marx et la révolution (*rires*) quand les étudiants doivent être notés. Ceux qui n'auront pas les notes suffisantes devront redoubler et payer encore plus ;

et s'ils redoublent trop de fois, ils devront aller balayer les rues. Il y a beaucoup de manières de perdre de vue ce qu'est l'université, une usine, une machine de sélection. La critique n'est pas tant ici que beaucoup à gauche, nous tous dans la mesure où nous acceptons de noter, acceptons le système, mais plutôt que nous prétendons ne pas y contribuer car nous enseignons des choses qui élèvent la conscience. Il n'y a pas eu aux États-Unis de luttes, des étudiants comme des professeurs, pour abolir le système des notes. Certains professeurs radicaux donnent des A à tout le monde mais ce n'est pas facile, à moins qu'il y ait une lutte. En Italie, dans les années 1970, les étudiants ont pu imposer la notation groupée. Ils n'ont pas pu abolir les notes, mais ils ont imposé d'être notés en tant que groupe. En gros, quinze, vingt personnes répondent collectivement à l'examen et reçoivent une seule note. Maintenant, ça a disparu mais c'était assez largement pratiqué.

Participant anonyme 1 : Y avait-il d'autres formes d'activités collaboratives parmi les étudiants à l'époque ?

SF : Oui, beaucoup. Par exemple, imposer un certain programme, décider ce qui allait être enseigné. Et il y avait la lutte pour le *pre-*

salario, le pré-salaire, qui est analogue au salaire étudiant.

JJ : Cette campagne, Des salaires pour les étudiants, était plus axée sur l'aspect économique de la vie étudiante. Contrairement aux années 1960, où on s'intéressait plus à la libération dans une perspective plus large : sexe, genre, race et beaucoup d'autres façons de comprendre la répression et la libération. Dans les années 1970, la lutte se recentra de nouveau autour de l'argent, du capital. Si on regarde la situation actuelle, bien pire en termes de droits étudiants et de condition sociale, je me demande par quelle mystification le capital a pu réussir à nous faire arriver là. Ça a été une opération bougrement significative de passer de l'éducation gratuite des années 1970 à l'esclavage par la dette d'aujourd'hui. Je me demande juste quels sont les mécanismes à l'oeuvre ici.

GC : Les mécanismes par lesquels cela est arrivé sont liés, d'une certaine manière, à la fin de la relation keynésienne entre les classes qui s'est développée dans les années 1950 et 1960 et qui est entrée en crise dans les années 1970. Ce qui s'est progressivement passé, c'est une transformation — pas seulement à l'université mais partout — de la sphère de la reproduction. Par exemple, ce qui est arrivé aux étudiants dans les années 1970 est similaire à ce qui s'est passé dans le domaine des aides sociales.

SF : Ce point est crucial. L'attaque contre l'inscription gratuite à la fac aux États-Unis a eu lieu en même temps que le début de l'attaque contre les aides sociales allouées aux femmes. Toutes les personnes bénéficiant d'une assistance de l'État, et surtout les femmes recevant l'AFDC (aide aux familles avec enfants à charge) ont été dénigrées. C'était un programme pour les mères isolées, qui recevaient un peu d'aide selon le principe qu'élever un enfant est un travail, et que la société bénéficiera de cet investissement dans les générations futures. Mais, à partir des années 1970, une campagne massive a été montée et elle dépréciait ces femmes qui vivaient de l'aide sociale, en les décrivant comme des parasites et des fraudeuses. Il y avait une forte composante raciste, car les femme qui se battaient pour les droits sociaux étaient en majorité noires, alors que pourtant la majorité des femmes vivant des aides sociales étaient blanches. C'était le début d'un long processus qui a mené en 1996 à l'abolition de l'ancien système d'aides sociales sous Clinton, et à un dénigrement accru des personnes bénéficiant de l'aide de la sécurité sociale. Aujourd'hui, dépendre de la sécurité sociale est présenté comme quelque chose de socialement destructeur — les personnes âgés sont pratiquement accusées de ruiner le pays et le futur des prochaines générations, même si l'argent de la sécurité sociale provient de leurs cotisations.

GC : Les étapes ont été nombreuses. La première, à l'université par exemple, a été la nouvelle façon d'organiser le financement qui a transformé totalement leur fonctionnement. Elles ont commencé à se transformer lentement en machines nourries par les droits d'inscriptions, telle une entreprise, alors même qu'elles se présentent comme des institutions publiques sans but lucratif. De cette façon, elles commencent à créer un environnement qui a sa propre logique. Dès lors que vous commencez à créer une situation où l'université ne peut se financer que sur la base des frais de scolarité, alors les frais augment constamment. Il y a quelque chose de mathématique là-dedans. Il n'y a pas d'échappatoire. On commence donc à avoir un type de système universitaire qui nous amène à la situation actuelle, elle-même intensifiée par la crise économique et financière. Et pour survivre à la crise, les universités doivent augmenter les frais d'inscriptions, ce qui crée des millions de micro-crises chez les étudiants et leurs familles.

JJ : George, tu a aussi mentionné ailleurs que, dans les années 1960, l'État investissait dans les universités, et qu'en retour, les étudiants se sont révoltés. En conséquence, dans les années 1970, l'État s'est retiré des campus. Ils ont compris que le capital réussirait mieux à discipliner que l'État. L'argent est la meilleure façon de discipliner les gens. Tu pourrais dire que c'était la conclusion des années 1960.

GC: Et cela a très bien fonctionné. La transformation des universités est bien claire pour tout le monde désormais. Notre critique de la vie menée par les étudiants est largement partagée. La question, maintenant, n'est plus celle de la critique mais plutôt de savoir ce qu'on en fait ; car la situation s'est radicalement retournée contre le pouvoir d'autodétermination des étudiants.

RG : Il y a dimension très intéressante dans ces deux luttes — celle pour le salaire au travail ménager et celle pour le salaire étudiant. Revendiquer un salaire pour une forme particulière de travail qui n'est pas considérée comme du travail, est une perspective d'une lutte qui pourrait remodeler totalement le champ de bataille. Parce que contrairement à ce que tu dis, George, ce n'est pas une vérité admise par tout le monde — je suis sûr que la plupart d'entre nous ne savaient rien de cette lutte pour le salaire étudiant, et je me demande quel élément de ce type de campagne aurait aujourd'hui un potentiel de mobilisation. Les luttes actuelles tendent à réagir contre, par exemple, la hausse des frais de scolarité. Quel est l'horizon des luttes actuelles ? Quel type de lutte pourrait changer le terrain de l'affrontement ou notre façon de voir la situation ? Notre perception de la situation semble en effet une partie du problème.

Alan Smart : Il transparaît dans la brochure que, dès la crise des années 1970, les « bons emplois » ne sont plus disponibles. On peut y voir les conséquences profondes de la situation post-industrielle de l'Occident. Maintenant, nous en voyons le résultat. Désormais, du moins de façon rhétorique, ce n'est pas seulement l'aide sociale qui est perçue comme une aumône parasitaire, mais le salaire en tant que tel. Le salarié qui s'attend à être payé à l'heure est un rabat- joie. Vous avez mentionné cette rhétorique « néo-entrepreneuriale », où chacun n'est pas seulement une petite entreprise mais aussi une « start-up », un « artiste », un « travailleur créatif ». Ce type de travail est entièrement reproductif ; le management est reproductif, la finance est reproductive. Dorénavant, ce qui est nié, supprimé, expatrié ou délocalisé en Chine,

c'est la véritable production. Si le travail reproductif du bout de la chaîne est le travail domestique, celui qui vous rend apte à travailler, à
l'autre bout on trouve la finance, le management
et le marketing, qui permettent à l'entreprise de
réussir. Il semble que le fossé entre les deux s'est
réduit, que nous sommes tous désormais des
entrepreneurs indépendants — nous travaillons
sur nos ordinateurs portables, en sous-vête-
ment, dans la chambre que nous louons et que
nous nettoyons tout en travaillant. Produire, ou
toucher un salaire pour son travail, voilà des
choses vulgaires qu'il ne faut pas mentionner.
Dans le boom des années 1990, si vous étiez
suffisamment exubérant et jeune, vous alliez
recevoir des fonds de Wall Street, vous alliez
percer et réussir, cela tomberait du Ciel. Ce
n'était pas la dette mais plutôt une action, un
risque. Maintenant, l'exploitation.

SF : Maintenant l'exploitation est cachée.

AS : J'ai comme une nostalgie pour la négati-
vité en puissance des salaires, là où le salarié
ne risque rien. Même si ceux pour qui vous
travaillez tirent beaucoup plus d'argent de votre
travail que vous, vous savez que s'ils ratent
leur pari, ou s'ils se plantent, ils devront quand
même vous payer. Alors que maintenant tout

est entrepreneurial, et on est censés faire des projets sur son temps libre. SF : Et on fait face au patron seul.

JJ : J'ai lu récemment un article sur une compagnie où 60 % des travailleurs sont stagiaires, ils n'ont pas de salaire. Et je me suis dit, si ça se trouve, dans dix ans, les stagiaires devront payer pour aller travailler (*rires*). C'est la même logique qu'à l'université. On nous dit que c'est un privilège que d'aller travailler. Il y aura donc bientôt des droits d'inscription, et vous aurez un job passionnant si vous avez de quoi payer.

SF : Ce sont les universités qui fournissent en flux tendu des stagiaires aux entreprises. De plus en plus de formations exigent de faire un stage. De cette manière, l'université peut extorquer du travail pas seulement de l'étudiant directement, mais aussi indirectement via le système de stage. On sait que des entreprises licencient leurs employés car les universités leur fournissent des stagiaires.

RG : Ça serait bien si des étudiants d'université — et je sais qu'il y en a ici puisque j'en connais certains — pouvaient essayer de relier certaines questions soulevées par le texte aux réalités et aux luttes actuelles.

Participant anonyme 2 : Quelques-uns d'entre nous sont à la Cooper Union. Je viens de finir mes études, et ce qui est arrivé en 1976 à la CUNY est en train de nous arriver actuellement. Donc la question de comment changer le terrain ou de comment y résister, de quel type de force nous disposons pour s'opposer aux frais de scolarité... Toute la communauté des anciens étudiants est opposée à la structure des frais de scolarité, mais ceux qui siègent au conseil d'administration sont tous des hommes d'affaires qui ne veulent rien avoir à faire avec nous, ils suivent un modèle capitaliste qu'ils qualifient de « réaliste ». C'est vraiment une question urgente pour nous. Donc si vous avez une réponse à cette question... (*Rires*).

Leo Caione : Je voudrais saisir l'occasion offerte par Rene. J'étais étudiant à Venise, je suis italien et ce que je voudrais dire au sujet de la brochure c'est qu'il y a beaucoup de changement avec le temps. Je peux donner une sorte de témoignage. Je ne veux pas parler de moi mais seulement utiliser mon expérience comme exemple, je suis anachronique car je viens d'une autre génération. Quand j'étais à l'école, je devais travailler pour pouvoir y aller. J'étais très jeune — onze ans. Maintenant les étudiants sont des enfants gâtés. Je vois que les étudiants ne donnent pas la même valeur que moi à la possibilité d'étudier. La brochure a bientôt quarante ans et le point de vue a beaucoup changé. À l'époque beaucoup de choses que dit le texte étaient peut-être vraies, mais maintenant les étudiants sont trop gâtés. Ils ne veulent rien faire !

Participant anonyme 3 : Il y a des enfants gâtés dans toutes les générations, je ne pense pas que tu puisses faire une telle généralisation.

LC : Je veux dire, il y a des professionnels aujourd'hui qui, pour pouvoir étudier, on fait des sacrifices dont nous n'avons pas idée.

Participant anonyme 4 : Il y a aussi eu un tournant, pour esquiver ce point de vue moral, c'est que l'espace de l'éducation est devenu transactionnel. Les étudiants considèrent que quelque chose leur est dû, car ils payent.

SF : Je suis désolé mais je travaille dans le système éducatif de ce pays depuis quarante ans et ce que tu décris n'a rien à voir avec mon expérience. Les étudiants auxquels j'ai enseignés travaillaient beaucoup et faisaient des sacrifices. Ils n'étaient pas gâtés. Si quelqu'un a trois jobs, en plus d'aller à l'école, pour pouvoir payer ses frais de scolarité et les autres coûts, il fait des sacrifices.

Participant anonyme 5 : Il y a quelque chose d'assez fascinant dans la façon dont on en est arrivé là, c'est-à-dire que leur éducation soit gratuite ou qu'ils payent 50 000 $ dans la Nouvelle École, les étudiants sont toujours caractérisés d'une manière ou d'une autre comme des enfants gâtés. C'est fascinant que cela s'applique dans tous les cas, que vous bénéficiez d'une éducation gratuite ou que vous ayez trois boulots et des milliers de dollars de dettes. Nous considérions autrefois qu'il y avait une sorte de droit à l'éducation que la société devait aux jeunes générations. C'est possible qu'il y ait des enfants gâtés, mais ce genre de discours ne fait qu'empêcher une analyse commune de l'exploitation au-delà des groupes sociaux, étudiants ou ouvriers.

Je n'avais jamais entendu parler de cette proposition de salaire étudiant. Je viens de Grande-Bretagne où il y a encore, ici et là, des occupations de fac en cours. Deux ans après les grandes vagues de manifs étudiantes, la lutte se poursuit. C'est exactement ce qu'il faut faire à un moment où les gens utilisent de plus en plus cette phraséologie populiste sur les privilégiés qui se retrouvent disciplinés et endettés. Surtout quand on vous dit : « Si tu veux aller dans cette voie-là, désormais il faudra que tu payes 9000 £

de frais de scolarité par an. » C'est la décadence. Même les journalistes de droite disent que le diplôme n'est plus un investissement viable. C'est une réponse fantastique, au moment même où ils commencent à multiplier par trois les frais d'inscription, de dire : « Nous allons plutôt demander des salaires pour ce travail. » Je pense que c'est une proposition politique saisissante. Je suis vraiment content d'avoir pu l'entendre lue à haute voix. Ça a dû être une expérience magnifique que de l'entendre ainsi (*rires*).

GC : Je vous assure que quand nous écrivions ce texte au coin d'une table dans notre cuisine, nous ne pensions pas qu'il pourrait être un sujet d'intérêt des décennies après. De toute façon, il y a des parties de cette histoire qui se sont déroulées entre 1975 et 2013 sur lesquelles il faut réfléchir. Je suis pas sûr que cela ait été dit jusqu'ici. Mais cela vaut le coup.

Participant anonyme 6 : J'ai le sentiment qu'il manque quelque chose à la discussion : la question du « que faire ? » Peut-on réexaminer la question de la valeur de l'éducation du point de vue du travailleur plutôt que de celui du capitaliste ? Je pense qu'il est important de comprendre la différence entre le processus de travail et celui d'éducation, et d'essayer de faire une distinction entre ces deux moments. Et ce, en relation avec cette idée d'étudiants gâtés ou de la manière dont la nature de l'éducation ellemême a changé ces quarante dernières années, et comment la marchandise éducative est consommée différemment entre hier et aujourd'hui. La production de cette marchandise dicte la façon dont elle est consommée par l'étudiant. Il me semble que revendiquer un salaire n'est pas nécessairement une bonne chose. On est toujours exploité quand on reçoit un salaire.

RG : Une partie de ces questions ont été abordées dans le texte que Silvia a écrit en 1974 « Des salaires contre le travail ménager. » Elle parle clairement du fait que le salaire n'est pas l'enjeu de la lutte. Parler de salaire c'est ouvrir un champ nouveau et comprendre ces relations complètement différemment. Donc il y a la question de l'éducation vis-à-vis du travail. D'une certaine manière, à cause de la forme intermittente du travail, qui participe de la façon dont le capitalisme fonctionne, vous devez constamment remettre en ordre ce que vous savez et comment vous le savez entre les moments où vous êtes payés, ce qui fait qu'apprendre est enchâssé dans le processus marchand et s'y adapte constamment. Peut-être que quelqu'un ici est déjà en train de préparer ses cours et est venu prendre des idées. On ne sait jamais ce qui va vous assurer un job, un concert ou je ne sais quoi encore. Il est beaucoup plus difficile de distinguer le travail de l'enseignement, alors que dans cette partie sur-développée du monde le travail nécessite de plus en plus de savoirs, qui eux-mêmes changent et s'adaptent à des circonstances en constante évolution.

JJ : Je pense que ce que George indiquait - le savoir est une discipline et ce discours sur les étudiants gâtés - provient du fait que les étudiants ont beaucoup de pouvoir au sein des universités car ils sont désormais des consommateurs. Les cours n'ont pas lieu s'il n'y a pas au moins dix étudiants qui s'y inscrivent. La hiérarchie du pouvoir au sein des universités a changé, du point de vue néolibéral elle est centrée autour de l'étudiant ; mais on pourrait dire aussi que cela fonctionne comme un dispositif disciplinaire, où les étudiants sont produits comme des consommateurs, et ils agissent en consommateurs puisqu'ils paient pour leurs études. Étudier dans ce contexte est une forme de discipline néolibérale. Ce changement dans la vision de l'étudiant, dans le sens « Je paye tant, je peux donc demander tant » structure l'université aujourd'hui.

Alexander Dwinell : Par rapport à cette idée « d'auto-investissement », il semble que la seule raison pour laquelle on étudie est de se préparer à travailler. Mais vous n'avez pas l'impression que beaucoup des qualifications que vous avez acquises à l'université ont un rapport direct avec ce que vous faites une fois au travail ? Et pourtant vous ne pouvez pas avoir ce job sans faire ce sacrifice physique ou vous endetter. De plus en plus, ça semble la seule raison pour laquelle les gens parlent de la valeur de l'éducation. Cela met des oeillères sur notre aptitude à discuter de la véritable valeur de l'éducation. Même avec la Cooper Union, on nous dit : « Il faut qu'on change les frais de scolarité car les marchés financiers ont changé et nous ne pouvons plus tout prendre à notre charge. » Sans jamais revenir sur aucune des raisons pour lesquelles il y a eu une éducation gratuite.

Participant anonyme 7 : C'est drôle comme le terme « gâté » revient dans la conversation. Au Québec, c'était la principale attaque des médias contre le mouvement étudiant, qu'ils étaient des enfants gâtés. C'est intéressant, car qu'est ce que c'est un enfant gâté ? Un enfant gâté est un enfant indiscipliné, qui ne fait pas ce qu'on lui demande, non ? C'est de là que vient l'expression et la voilà importée pour parler d'étudiants en troisième cycle. J'ai enseigné à beaucoup d'étudiants qui restent assis au fond et se plaignent : « Le voilà qui reparle de Marx. » C'est très tentant de les considérer comme gâtés, mais j'ai commencé à y réfléchir et à parler avec eux et ils achètent une éducation. Ils achètent une bonne référence. La plupart des étudiants avec lesquels j'ai parlé ont le sentiment que les éléments critiques du programme scolaire allaient les empêcher d'être performants plutôt de les aider. Et si cette « paresse », cette « indiscipline » était une forme de résistance rudimentaire qu'il faut organiser ? Et s'il s'agissait de dire : « Franchement, la société dans laquelle je vais obtenir ce diplôme n'en a rien à foutre de moi, donc pourquoi devrais-je m'en préoccuper ? Qu'est-ce que je dois à ces gens ? Pourquoi devrais-je travailler dur ? » C'est très tentant de penser que nous devrions militer avec les étudiants enthousiastes et naïfs qui s'investissent vraiment dans les études. Mais je pense qu'on devrait travailler avec la vaste majorité des étudiants dans le système actuellement — qui ne sont pas gâtés mais incroyablement exploités et disciplinés. Le problème n'est pas que les étudiants ne sont pas assez disciplinés, c'est qu'il ne sont pas assez en colère.

RG : Je pense qu'on perd de vue un aspect du problème, c'est-à-dire, comme le dit Leo, la dimension de classe. Il est facile d'écarter cette question des « étudiants gâtés », mais même dans ma propre expérience, venant d'un milieu immigré pauvre, la première fois que j'ai été à l'université, je me suis dit : « Je suis entouré d'enfants gâtés. » J'ai ressenti un poids énorme dans le genre : « Les gens ont vécu une vie de merde pour que je sois dans cette école pour supposément en vivre une meilleure. » Cette situation forme vraiment la façon dont vous percevez les gens autour de vous, et je comprends comment, étant moi-même dans cette position, vous voyez les autres comme opposés à vous ou n'ayant aucun sens du réel. On peut parler de ces étudiants qui travaillent dur ou au contraire de cette posture privilégiée qui a quelque chose d'une résistance. Ces deux aspects existent, mais néanmoins il y a une séparation entre les classes, dans le sens où ceux qui viennent de milieux aisés et ceux qui viennent de milieux ouvriers et immigrés ne perçoivent pas l'université de la même manière — cela ne vient pas de nulle part. Donc il est facile pour ceux qui voient des gosses de riches occuper le hall de la fac de les considérer comme quantités négligeables et de dire : « Ils peuvent faire ça parce que leurs parents sont riches et moi à la fin de la journée, il faut que j'aille travailler et j'ai plein de merdes à gérer, des factures, des dettes . . . » C'est aussi contre cela que nous luttons. On ne peut pas écarter de façon rhétorique cette division, mais on doit trouver un moyen de la prendre à bras le corps. Et ça peut être compliqué quand tu as eu l'expérience de la grande pauvreté ailleurs et que tu arrives là et te dis : « C'est un endroit super, il y a beaucoup plus d'opportunités pour moi que de là où je viens. » Je ne suis pas d'accord quand on dit que tous les étudiants sont gâtés mais nous devons reconnaître que la classe est un problème majeur.

LC : Je ne veux pas qu'on se méprenne sur ce que j'ai dit à propos des étudiants gâtés. Je sais juste qu'il y a des gens comme moi qui ont dû faire trois boulots en même temps pour aller à l'université.

AA : Mais la discussion porte sur l'ensemble de la situation. Tu dis : « Je ne veux pas me mettre au centre. » C'est important de ne pas rester rivé à son expérience. De penser avec les autres. « Qui sont les autres avec qui je peux réfléchir ? Comment puis-je changer la situation ? »

GC : Dans les quarante années qui séparent la publication de cette brochure et aujourd'hui, j'ai pu voir de mes yeux et sentir dans mes tripes la défaite de la politique prônée par ce texte et les conséquences de cette défaite. Cela m'a pris du temps pour comprendre les conséquences profondes pour mes étudiants. À partir de la fin des années 1990, et au début de ce siècle, mes étudiants, qui sont dans une université populaire du Maine, non seulement devaient payer pour des frais de scolarité qui ont commencé à augmenter bien plus vite que l'inflation, mais ont aussi commencé à être confrontés à un endettement qui était nouveau pour eux et leurs familles. Je n'ai pas eu conscience de cette transformation pendant de nombreuses années. Je ne voyais pas ce qui arrivait à mes propres étudiants. J'étais le bon prof radical, qui passait des nuits à noter des étudiants selon leur compréhension de la notion d'aliénation du travail chez Marx, sans reconnaître le fait que ces étudiants devaient payer des dettes énormes pour pouvoir assister à mon cours et étudier l'aliénation. Ces dernières années, j'ai commencé à faire pénitence, je me suis consacré à essayer de changer cela. J'ai fait ce que j'ai pu, avec quelques camarades présents ici, dans la campagne Occupy Student Debt et dans d'autres initiatives comme la grève de la dette pour mettre en évidence cette question. Je parle d'une situation qui s'est généralisée pour la majeure partie des étudiants qui, pour aller à la fac, doivent toujours plus s'endetter. Cela a des conséquences, pour ce que je peux voir, extrêmement démobilisantes. Si la lutte actuelle contre la dette étudiante et l'éducation gratuite échoue, toute une génération ne sera pas en mesure d'organiser une lutte autonome contre le capital. La première étape pour changer cette situation est de changer la relation entre ceux qui ont des dettes étudiantes et ceux qui les tiennent dans leurs griffes. Dans cette discussion, il est vital qu'avant de commencer à revendiquer un salaire pour les étudiants, il faut se débarrasser de la dette à laquelle on les astreint actuellement.

JJ : Un des axes de la brochure s'oppose à l'éducation. Je reste perplexe devant le fait que tant d'étudiants — nous tous d'une certaine manière — vont consciemment à l'université, l'usine disciplinaire, sachant très bien ce qui va arriver.

GC : Notre but était de transformer l'aliénation en pouvoir. En d'autres termes, au lieu de considérer l'aliénation comme un vecteur de défaite, nous essayions, en transformant les études en une relation salariale, d'un côté de reconnaître le travail scolaire comme une exploitation et de l'autre faire reconnaître cette aliénation. En un sens, oui, *Des salaires pour les étudiants* est contre l'éducation. Mais il y a une autre ironie là-dedans, puisque c'est dans ce processus d'aliénation que tu apprends ce qu'est la lutte et que tu peux commencer à lutter.

JJ : La lutte *est* une école. L'éducation est une lutte, pas une soumission.

GC : Exactement . . . Des choses similaires sont à l'oeuvre dans le travail reproductif domestique.

JJ : Chers amis de la Cooper Union, je me demandais : est ce que vous discutez du fait de quitter la fac ou de dire merde à l'école ? Ou d'organiser les étudiants et faire votre propre école ?

Participant anonyme 8 : C'est plutôt vers ça que je pencherais, mais nous n'avons pas pour l'instant envisagé des futurs possibles.

Victoria Sobel : Je viens d'un milieu similaire et je suis des cours dans une université gratuite. Je viens pour moitié d'une migration de première génération et pour l'autre de deuxième génération. Je pense que faire une analyse de classe de ce qui se passe est crucial. Il y a deux choses en jeu. Il y a la stratification entre ceux qui peuvent se permettre d'aller étudier et ceux qui doivent s'endetter. Pour parler des luttes étudiantes, je suis d'accord que l'accès à l'université est une question de classe. C'est intéressant ce que vous disiez sur les étudiants privilégiés occupant les halls. Dans mon cas et dans le cas de beaucoup de mes pairs, c'était plutôt l'opposé. J'étais peut-être une des étudiantes les plus pauvres et les plus marginalisées. Je ne suis pas dans un endroit où je peux permettre que ça continue. On voit les deux côtés, les étudiants les plus endettés et ceux qui ont de l'espace, qui ont toujours eu de l'espace, se lever. Il s'agit d'unifier ceux qui réclament de l'espace, ce que nous essayons, je crois, de faire dans notre école, ou bien créer quelque chose de nouveau.

Graeme Thompson : Si l'éducation dans le cadre de l'institution devient une marchandise dont les rendements sont décroissants si on les rapporte à la dette, cela soulève la question : l'éducation ne devrait-elle pas sortir de l'institution ? Du moins pour ce qui est de l'éducation que nous considérons comme valable. Il semble qu'on s'enfonce de manière suicidaire dans l'endettement. Surtout quand on se questionne de plus en plus sur l'intérêt d'avoir un diplôme. Ça ne mène à rien et il n'y a plus d'horizon d'émancipation. Alors pourquoi les gens associent-ils toujours l'éducation à l'université si la valeur qu'on peut en retirer s'évanouit ?

SF : Dans beaucoup de cas, c'est par désespoir, car on ne peut pas trouver de travail sans un certain diplôme. Même si vous n'avez que peu de chances de trouver un travail avec, vous savez que c'est ce que vous devez faire. Il n'y a pas beaucoup de choix. C'est pour cela que les gens continuent à vouloir ce diplôme et paient pour, espérant que ça va leur amener un peu de sécurité.

AD : Je pense qu'il y a aussi le facteur des universités privées dans cette lutte. Je ne pense pas qu'on en ait assez parlé dans cette discussion. C'est là qu'une part significative de la dette étudiante a été contractée pour des diplômes ayant souvent encore moins de valeur. C'est comme les saisies immobilières, du genre : « D'accord. On étend votre crédit pour une courte période pour que vous soyez complètement englouti dans ce système et ensuite nous allons tout vous voler, et il faudra quand même nous rembourser. » Ça piège totalement les gens et élimine la possibilité de réfléchir plus loin que la survie quotidienne.

Themis Pellas : Je ne sais pas si certains d'entre vous étaient dans le syndicat étudiant qui a tenu quelques réunions au dernier semestre, mais nous avons discuté pour savoir comment aller au-delà d'un syndicat étudiant et créer un syndicat de travailleurs à l'échelle de la ville. Ce qui veut dire qu'il faut comprendre qu'étudiants et travailleurs passent d'un côté comme de l'autre, qu'il ne faut pas oublier que l'université les prépare pour les professions qui sont à l'extérieur. Donc il faut travailler des deux côtés, et aussi entre les deux. Comment intervenir dans cette situation complexe ? En intervenant sur toutes ces positions, je dirais. Ce qui veut dire créer la profession que tu souhaites exercer tandis que tu es à l'université. Il y a une chose intéressante dans Occupy, car des gens de diverses universités essayent de penser en terme d'intérêt mutuel : « Comment puis-je leur être utile ? » Si je veux aller au-delà de ces institutions, il faut que je change. Nous avons besoin de ces luttes élargies.

SF : C'est utile de faire parallèle entre l'éducation et la santé, car on peut faire le même raisonnement. On peut dire : « Il y a beaucoup de gens riches qui n'en n'ont pas besoin, donc nous n'avons pas besoin d'un système de santé universel. » De fait, les gens utilisent ce argument tout le temps. Mais on peut dire aussi : « Nous devrions créer un système de santé hors du marché. » Les gens essaient de créer des alternatives car ils savent que les soins que nous recevons sont de mauvaise qualité. Néanmoins nous ne pouvons pas abandonner le système médical tel qu'il est parce que nous n'avons pas pour l'instant les moyens de le remplacer. Je vois les luttes de l'éducation et de la santé comme faisant partie d'un même processus. Il y a différentes manières pour commencer à les changer. Si nous les voyons comme définitivement figées, nous sommes perdus. Les étudiants ne sont pas seuls, nous devons voir leurs luttes dans un contexte plus large. Sinon, nous ne pouvons pas dépasser les tactiques particulières et c'est une défaite.

JJ : Juste une chose au sujet de l'éducation autogérée. Nous avions l'université libre de Copenhague et l'État a fait une loi pour la rendre illégale, nous interdisant d'utiliser le terme université. Le capital a peur que les étudiants commencent à développer leurs propres idées en vue d'organiser leurs propres universités. Et même si nous n'existons plus désormais — on a fermé en 2007 — nous avons cette lettre nous disant que si nous envisageons de rouvrir cette université, elle serait illégale. Toutes ces petites choses s'ajoutent.

Common Notions is a publishing house and and programming machine that fosters the collective formulation of new directions for living autonomy in everyday life. We aim to translate, produce, and circulate tools of knowledge production utilized in movement-building practices. Through a variety of media, we seek to generalize common notions about the creation of other worlds beyond state and capital. Our publications trace a constellation of historical, critical, and visionary meditations on the organization of both domination and its refusal. Inspired by various traditions of autonomism—in the U.S. and internationally, historical and emerging from contemporary movements—we aim to provide tools of militant research in our collective reading of struggles past, present, and to come. Common Notions regularly collaborates with editorial houses, political collectives, militant authors, and visionary designers around the world. Our political and aesthetic interventions are dreamt and realized in collaboration with Antumbra Designs.

www.commonnotions.org
info@commonnotions.org

vaticanochico is a group of three friends, pontificating as a small but grand institution, which seeks to restitute curiosity as a generalized mode of relation with the world. vaticanochico proclaims itself a tartamuda (stuttering) institution, one that believes in trying things out at least twice. Tartamuda means the stubborn insistence in slowly making things familiar. vaticanochico poses close encounters as an informal work methodology, in which we take advantage of intimate and remote friendships—personal and professional—to give form to that which we would like to see, and have, closer. vaticanochico is the name of a neighborhood in Santiago, Chile, where its founding members live, it is also the name we give our provincial working logic and its delusions of grandeur. vaticanochico are engaged and inquisitive researchers that will publish, exhibit and bring within reach all that we consider worthwhile and necessary to spend more time with.

www.vaticanochico.com

Common Notions es una casa editorial y máquina de programación que incita la formulación colectiva de nuevas direcciones para vivir la autonomía en la cotidianidad. Pretendemos traducir, producir y circular herramientas de producción de conocimiento utilizadas para la construcción de movimientos y sus prácticas. A través de una diversidad de medios, buscamos generalizar nociones comunes sobre la creación de otros mundos, más allá del Estado y el capital. Nuestras publicaciones delinean una constelación de meditaciones históricas, críticas y visionarias acerca de los modos de dominación y su rechazo. Inspirados por varias tradiciones de autonomismo —en los Estados Unidos e internacionalmente— pretendemos proveer herramientas de investigación militante en nuestra lectura colectiva de luchas pasadas, presentes y las que vendrán. Common Notions colabora regularmente con casas editoriales, colectivos políticos, autores militantes y diseñadores visionarios del mundo entero. Nuestras intervenciones políticas y estéticas son soñadas y realizadas en colaboración con Antumbra Designs.

www.commonnotions.org
info@commonnotions.org

vaticanochico es un grupo de tres amigos auto pontificados como una pequeña-gran institución que busca la restitución de la curiosidad como modo de relación generalizada con el mundo. vaticanochico se proclama a sí mismo una institución tartamuda que cree en probar las cosas unas cuantas veces. Tartamuda significa la obstinada insistencia en lentamente hacer que las cosas se vuelvan familiares. vaticanochico plantea el encuentro como metodología de trabajo informal, en que aprovechamos nuestros vínculos de amistad locales y remotas —personales y profesionales— para darle forma a aquello que queremos ver y tener cerca. vaticanochico es el nombre de un barrio ubicado en Santiago de Chile en que viven sus miembros fundadores. Es el nombre que le damos a nuestra lógica de funcionamiento provinciana reconociendo sus inflados aires de grandeza. vaticanochico somos investigadores inquisitivos, comprometidos con publicar, exponer y traer todo aquello que merece una atención especial y con lo que creemos necesario pasar más rato.

www.vaticanochico.com

Common Notions est une maison d'édition et une machine programmée pour favoriser la formulation collective de nouvelles orientations pour vivre l'autonomie au quotidien. Nous visons à traduire, produire et diffuser des outils de production de connaissances utilisées dans les pratiques de constructions et de renforcement des mouvements. Grâce à une variété de médias, nous cherchons à rendre communes quelques notions au sujet de la création d'autres mondes au-delà de l'État et du capital. Nos publications dessinent une constellation de méditations historiques, critiques et visionnaires sur l'organisation tant de la domination que de son refus. Inspiré par diverses traditions de l'autonomie – aux États-Unis et à l'étranger, historiquement et dans les mouvements les plus contemporains - nous espérons fournir des outils de recherche militante dans notre lecture collective des luttes passées, présentes et à venir. « Notions communes » collabore régulièrement avec d'autres maisons d'éditions, des collectifs politiques, des auteurs militants et des graphistes utopistes du monde entier. Nos interventions politiques et esthétiques sont rêvées et réalisées en collaboration avec Antumbra Designs.

www.commonnotions.org
info@commonnotions.org

vaticanochico est un groupe de trois amis, pontifié comme une petite mais grandiose institution, qui cherche à refaire de la curiosité un rapport habituel au monde. Vaticanochico veut être une institution tartamuda (bégaiement), celui qui croit en essayant des choses au moins deux fois. Tartamuda signifie faire avec l'insistance têtue qui fait lentement devenir toutes choses familières. Vaticanochico marche au gré des rencontres et les méthodes de travail informel qu'elles exigent, où les amitiés intimes et éloignées – personnelles et professionnelles - permettent de donner forme à ce que nous aimerions voir exister et tenir autour de nous. Vaticanochico c'est le nom d'un quartier de Santiago, au Chili, où ses membres fondateurs vivent, et c'est aussi le nom que nous donnons à notre logique de travail provincial et ses illusions de grandeur. Vaticanochico nous fait être chercheurs, enquêteurs, engagés et curieux, compromis avec l'édition, pour publier, exposer et partager tout ce qui mérite une attention particulière, un intéressement par lequel créer ce avec quoi il nous importe de vivre aujourd'hui et pour longtemps.

www.vaticanochico.com

More from Common Notions

Colectivo Situaciones
19 & 20: Notes for a New Social Protagonism
(with Autonomedia)

Selma James
Sex, Race, and Class—The Perspective of Winning:
A Selection of Writings 1952–2011
(with PM Press)

Silvia Federici
Revolution at Point Zero:
Housework, Reproduction, and Feminist Struggle
(with PM Press)

George Caffentzis
In Letters of Blood and Fire:
Work, Machines, and the Crisis of Capitalism
(with PM Press)

Strike Debt
The Debt Resisters' Operations Manual
(with PM Press)

Mariarosa Dalla Costa and Monica Chilese
Our Mother Ocean: Enclosure, Commons,
and the Global Fishermen's Movement

Mariarosa Dalla Costa
Family, Welfare, and the State:
Between Progressivism and the New Deal